Realistic Track Plans for O Gauge Trains

Martin J. McGuirk

KALMBACH
BOOKS

ABOUT THE AUTHOR

Associate Editor Marty McGuirk joined the *Model Railroader* magazine staff in early 1996 after spending a year and a half at sister magazine *Classic Toy Trains*. Marty has been a model railroader since he was 8 years old, starting with a Lionel set before switching to HO scale in his early teens.

Before coming to Kalmbach, Marty spent 8 years on active duty in the U.S. Navy. His service included the Persian Gulf War and assignment to Washington, D.C., as Technical Editor for the AEGIS Shipbuilding Program. While doing all that he managed to find the time to start the Central Vermont Railway Historical Society in 1988.

Moving to Wisconsin meant disassembling his Central Vermont layout. The Central Vermont may ride again, but currently he is hard at work on a smaller scale layout based on the Western Maryland. His other interests include golf, fly-fishing, and spending time with his three sons, Jeff, Séan, and Matt.

Printed in the United States of America

97 98 99 00 01 02 03 04 05 06   10 9 8 7 6 5 4 3 2 1

For more information, visit our website at http://www.kalmbach.com

Publisher's Cataloging-in-Publication
(Provided by Quality Books, Inc.)

McGuirk, Martin
    Realistic track plans for O gauge trains / Martin McGuirk. —
1st ed.
    p. cm.
    Includes bibliographical references.
    ISBN 0-89778-434-0

    1. Railroads—Models.   I. Title.

TF197.M34 1997   625.1'9
                                  QBI97-646

Book design: Mark Watson
Cover design: Kristi Ludwig
Track plan colorization: Terri Metzger

CONTENTS

What makes a track plan realistic?

Before discussing what makes a plan realistic, perhaps we should address why an O gauge layout should *be* "realistic." After all, traditional O gauge layouts are arranged on tabletops with lots of track, accessories, and perhaps a little scenery. But model railroading and the toy train hobby have undergone a great deal of change over the last few years. O gauge toy trains are more realistic than ever before. Increasing interest in the O scale hobby has led to the greater availability of more and more details, figures, structure kits, and landscaping material, many of which are suitable for use by toy train layout builders. This in turn has resulted in the increasing popularity of a whole new segment of the toy train hobby that has come to be known as hi-rail.

Hi-rail layouts blend the operating advantages and sheer fun of toy trains with the realistic scenery, structures, and details of scale model railroads. Hi-rail layouts are nothing new—even the earliest Lionel catalogs illustrated toy trains in realistic settings—but in the last 10 years an explosion of products and the increasing realism of toy trains have made hi-rail layouts easier than ever to build. Today's O gauge equipment is more realistic than ever before. In many cases, the only things that give the model away as a "toy" are the large wheel flanges and oversized couplers.

In spite of all these improvements, many toy train operators, even hi-railers, continue to operate their trains on layouts with outdated designs and concepts. With the increased realism in rolling stock and locomotives, it's time to look at the next logical step in the evolution of the toy train hobby—more realistic track plans.

Toy train operators certainly don't have to give up the "magic" of toy trains in favor of scale model railroaders' "prototypically correct" layout plans, but while model railroaders aren't minding the store, let's borrow, steal, or otherwise adapt some of their principles to toy train layout design.

The secret to a realistic track plan, no matter what gauge or scale you model, doesn't relate to cost or skill. What is it? A theme.

That's right—the key to a realistic track plan and layout is a strong theme. There's also no "right" or "wrong" theme. If this is so subjective, why waste time worrying about it? Simply put, the existence of a theme makes a layout easier for visitors to understand. And if you don't really care what visitors think, that same central theme benefits you. It gives you a framework to hang your efforts on so work can proceed at a steady pace and the desired result, an interesting and attractive model railroad, will be much easier to achieve.

But a theme isn't as simple as picking a prototype railroad. It's ridiculous to choose "the Santa Fe" as a theme for layout unless you're building it in the main concourse of Grand Central terminal.

The theme of the railroad should be reflected in the track plan. A single-track main line with weed-grown ballast would look strange if the railroad was supposed to be the New York Central along the Hudson River, just as a multitrack railroad under catenary would look out of place in a setting reminiscent of the Mojave Desert.

A definite theme was the starting point for each plan in this book. I've tried to choose interesting railroads to start with, then selected aspects of their operation, scenery, or equipment to feature.

While you should feel free to build any of these layouts as shown, I'd be more pleased if you would use some of the track arrangements and ideas to develop a toy train layout that's your very own. And if you do build one of these railroads, please share the results with *Classic Toy Trains*.

Introduction to Realistic Layout Design

There's something fascinating, even mesmerizing, about watching a miniature train negotiate its way through a maze of track, switches, and curves. Special track arrangements and combinations of switches allow an amazing variety of train movements and add a great deal of visual appeal to any layout.

While no one facet of the hobby is more important than another, nothing is quite as fascinating as switches and track arrangements that let you duplicate the movements of freight and passenger trains. A plausible track plan adds realism to any layout. Suddenly those prized engines aren't simply running around the basement. They're taking the siding to meet the *Lionel Limited,* working the yard late at night classifying cars for the *MTH Midnight Manifest,* or winding their way through intricate waterfront trackage. In a blink of an eye, you're not just building a layout, you're creating a miniature world. There are many ways to describe any track plan, but the most basic and fundamental is the schematic.

LAYOUT SCHEMATICS

A schematic is the basic route of the layout's main line. No matter how many

**Continuous-run
schematic**

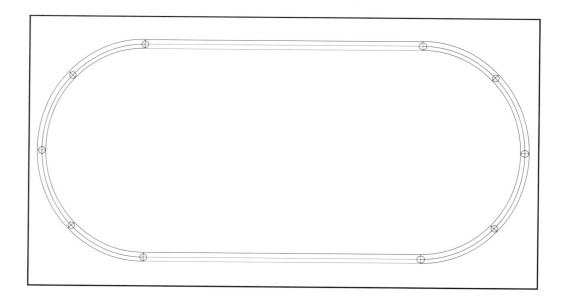

extra tracks and optional routes you include in a plan, you should still be able to distill the plan into a basic schematic.

While it's not required, sometimes it's a good idea to start with the schematic before you design the plan. Which schematic you choose says a lot about how you view layout design. The type of operation you prefer will really determine the schematic you'll use.

If you like to just sit back and watch 'em roll, you'll most likely be happiest with a schematic that lets you do that, such as an oval, loop to loop, or twice around.

On the other hand, operators who prefer the challenges of switching will be happier with an out-and-back or point-to-point arrangement.

Continuous-run: In simple language, the continuous-run layout is a circle or an oval. This is the most basic schematic and the one many of us start with. We all love to watch the train go around, and manufacturers know that. That's why just about

every train set comes with a circle or an oval of track.

In some cases, the oval can give the impression of a train chasing its tail endlessly in circles. However, over the years, model railroaders have become quite adept at disguising the round-and-round nature of the oval track plan. Trains wind in and out, up and down on various levels with no apparent repetition.

Point-to-point: Real railroads don't make money running around in circles. They run trains from point A to point B, stopping at other points between. The simplest point-to-point layout would have track running in a straight line from one side of the room to the other. While this schematic gives you the closest simulation of the prototype, it has one disadvantage. First, on all but the largest railroads the run will be too short to seem realistic. Just when the run seems to have started, it's time to turn around and head back the other way. The second big

**Point-to-point
schematic**

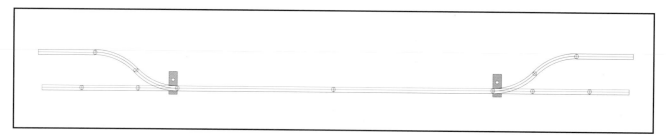

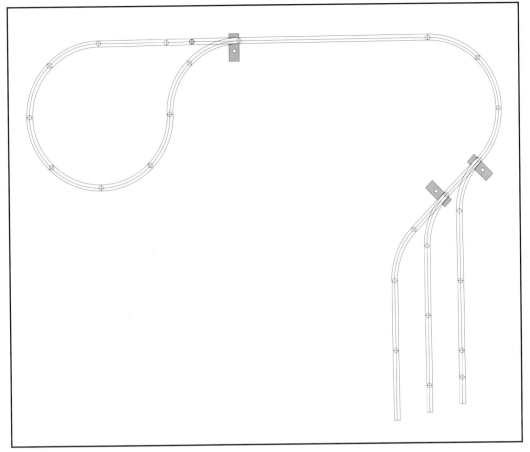

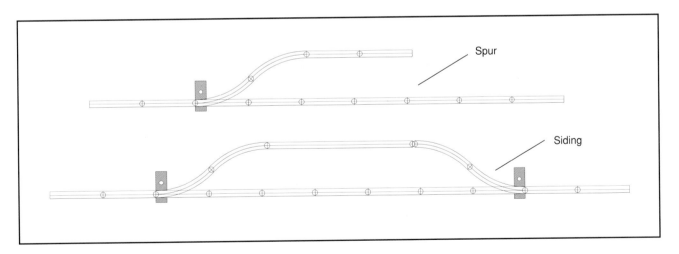

Spur

Siding

disadvantage with a strict point-to-point layout is the need to turn engines at both ends of the run.

Out-and-back: This is point-to-point layout with one terminal serving as both ends of the run. Trains leave the terminal, travel over a stretch of track representing miles of countryside, and return to the same terminal they started from. Only this time, the terminal is "miles" away.

There are almost unlimited possibilities for model railroad track arrangements, but all railroads have their basis in one, or some combination of one or more, of these three basic schematics.

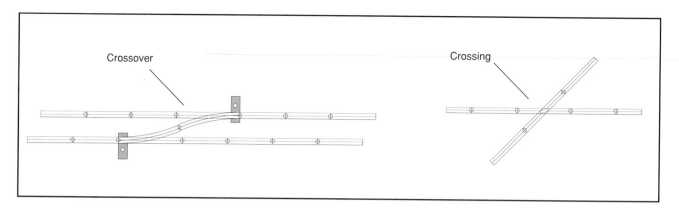

Crossover

Crossing

Crossing and crossover schematic

ADDING INTEREST TO A TRACK PLAN

Once you've decided on a schematic, what elements can make a track plan more interesting? After all, your cars and locomotives are based on real railroad equipment and your scenery depicts the real hills, rocks, and trees from your favorite area of the country. So why shouldn't the track arrangements duplicate those found on real railroads?

Real railroads are made up of miles and miles of fairly uneventful trackage highlighted with areas of real interest such as terminals, yards, interchanges with other railroads, and junctions with branch lines. These interest areas are the ideal inspiration for any track planner to focus on since they cram much more activity (and in model railroading increased activity equals increased interest) into fairly compact areas.

But even the main line features interesting segments. Sidings allow trains to pass one another, and spurs or industrial sidings facilitate dropping off and picking up freight cars for the railroad's customers. You'll want to include some examples of each of these track types in your layout plan. Once again, although the possibilities are endless, there are only two basic types of side tracks for the purposes of our discussion: spurs and sidings.

The spur is the simplest of all track arrangements, a single switch leading to a dead-end track. Spurs are frequently located within towns or near stations, and the track may serve one or more customers.

If the spur doesn't dead-end but connects back into the main line through a

Wye and reverse loop schematic

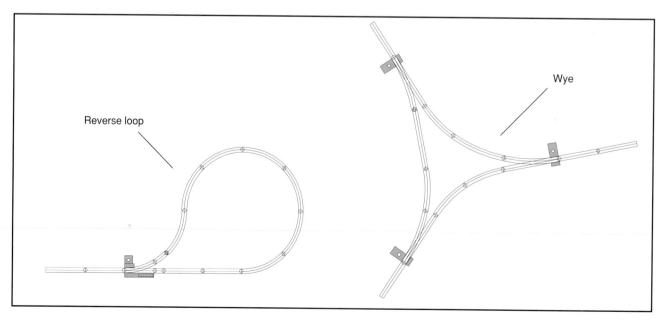

Reverse loop

Wye

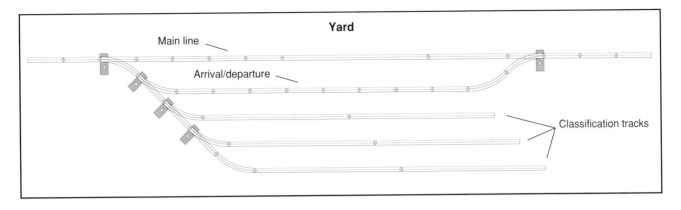

Yard

Main line

Arrival/departure

Classification tracks

Yard schematic

second switch, then it's called a siding. Passing sidings are the key to single-track railroads. A slower train can take the siding to allow a faster train to pass. Or an eastbound train can sit on the siding, clearing the main line for a westbound train.

Double-ended sidings are also frequently found in yards on arrival tracks. In this case, the siding serves as an engine escape track to make it easy to move the locomotive into the engine servicing area.

Other key track arrangements are crossings and crossovers. Although the names sound alike, they are quite different. Crossovers are found on multitrack lines. They permit a train to go from one track to another. A crossing allows one track to cross another at an angle. On the model train layout, the crossover consists of two or four switches in tandem or combination, whereas the crossing is accomplished using a prefabricated unit. The most common crossings have 45- and 90-degree components, although other angles are available.

REVERSING SECTIONS: REVERSE LOOPS AND WYES

In many cases you'll want to send a train back to where it started traveling in the opposite direction. This requires the use of a reversing section. Don't let the name confuse you: a reversing section is made up of a number of individual track components. The most common reversing sections are the wye and the reverse loop.

A wye is a triangular arrangement of track made up of three legs, one of which may be the main line. The wye permits

reversing a single engine, or an entire train, depending on the length of the leg. Prototype railroads use wyes frequently at points where branches join the main and in engine terminals.

A reversing loop is another neat track arrangement. It's not as common on the prototype as we might like, but real world reverse loops (prototype railroads call them "balloon tracks") aren't unheard of. As we already discussed, the reverse loop is the secret to the out-and-back track schematic. I've used reverse loops with many of the plans in this book.

YARDS

Yards are both a blessing and a curse to the layout designer. On the one hand, they are neat places to look at trains, and there's much to be said for a real world situation that crams as much track as possible into a given space. After all, that's what many of our layouts end up looking like, isn't it? But real yards, especially nowadays, are huge affairs covering hundreds of acres and operating many miles of track. So does that mean yards can't be included in a toy train layout? Of course not. It's simply a matter of boiling the yard's functions down into a manageable size, and ignoring many of the extra tracks that contribute little, if anything, to the operating interest of your layout. First, it's important to understand how a real yard works.

All real trains start and end their journeys in a yard. In their simplest terms, prototype yards are sorting and distribution facilities. For example, if a train

comes into Cleveland, the cars in the train could be heading for hundreds of individual destinations. The yard crew sorts the individual cars based on their final destinations. All the cars, for example, heading to Atlanta would be placed on one track, the Chicago cars on another track, and Pittsburgh-bound cars on a third. As other trains arrive, their cars will also be re-sorted according to destination, and when enough cars have been accumulated to make up a train, a train will be dispatched. (Of course, the actual process, with thousands of destinations and hundreds of thousands of cars is far more complicated, but you get the idea.)

Yards tracks may look alike but there are different kinds of tracks that serve different, and important, functions. Two of the most significant tracks are arrival/departure tracks and classification tracks.

Arrival/departure tracks allow trains to enter and leave the yard limits without interfering with the yard crews. Once the road crew brings the engine into the yard, they turn the power over to the hostler, who moves the locomotives to the servicing area. Once the power is clear, the yard crews place the caboose (back in the days of cabooses) onto the caboose track and move the just-arrived cars to the classification tracks for sorting.

Classification tracks serve as sorting bins, giving yard crews the space they need to arrange individual cars into cuts for moving to their next stop. In addition to the tracks already mentioned, yards include other tracks you may want to consider adding, depending upon the space you have and your interest. These include RIP (repair-in-place) tracks for cars awaiting minor repairs, cleaning tracks for cleaning cars before they are sent to a shipper for loading, and storage tracks. Years ago, yards included other tracks that technology has rendered obsolete, such as icing tracks for loading the ice bunkers in refrigerator cars and coaling tracks for delivery of coal to the locomotive terminal and coal cars.

The possibilities for yard arrangements are almost endless. I advise you to spend some time looking at real small railroad yards in and around your hometown. Before you venture onto railroad property, keep in mind that railroads are private property, and many frown upon, and prosecute, unauthorized trespassers. Be sure to ask for permission before setting foot on railroad property. In many cases you'll be asked to sign a release. It's best to find an overpass or public area adjacent to a yard. That way you can still check out the action and stay safe and legal. Even a small facility can add interest to your layout. As a matter of fact, the smaller the real yard, the more useful it will be to your track planning—but even large facilities can be adapted to model railroad use if you reduce track lengths and reduce the sheer number of classification tracks and the like.

PUTTING IT TOGETHER

Once you've found the perfect theme for your layout and you are familiar with the various schematics and possible track arrangements, it's time to get to work.

The first step in planning the track for anything beyond a small 4 x 8-foot tabletop layout is to create an accurate scale drawing of the space you have to work with. Don't fudge the dimensions here—any lies will come back to haunt you when you find your dream layout just doesn't fit the space.

You can draw the track plan using the traditional pencil-and-paper method or with plastic templates like the ones made by CTT, Inc.

The templates make it easy to determine exactly what will or won't fit in the space you have available.

In recent years a number of computer programs specifically made for toy train track planning have become available. My favorite, and the one I used for the plans in this book, is called RR-Track. This program is fairly easy to work with once you get used to it, and it includes libraries for all the popular brands of track, as well as a large number of accessories.

WALK-IN OR TABLETOP?

Once you know how much space you have available, it's decision time again. Just as track plans can be boiled down to one of three basic schematics, how the layout fits in the room is really a choice between a walk-in arrangement, a tabletop or island-style layout, and a donut. Other planners have described layout styles in various degrees of detail in layout design books over the years, but for our purposes these three will suffice.

The island, or tabletop, layout is by far the most common style of layout among toy train operators.

As the name implies, the tabletop is just that—it's a large, usually flat, table that fills the floor space in the center of the room (hence the name *island*). This style of construction is easy to build, and there's no denying that it's fun to stand back and watch the trains snake their way through a scene. But there are two potential disadvantages that may stand in the way of enjoying the layout. First, access can become quite difficult, especially if the table gets wider than 6 feet across. While the trains will stay on the track without a great deal of trouble, especially if you've used the proper amount of care in laying the track, accessories placed in the center of the table are notorious for requiring constant attention. It's Murphy's Law at work—the accessory or switch most difficult to reach will be the one requiring the most attention.

But many toy train operators continue to favor the island-style layout, and with reasons that go beyond nostalgia for department store displays. Many operators—close to 70 percent, if the *Classic Toy Trains* survey is to be believed—are also collectors. They like to display their prized pieces on shelves to share with family, friends, and fellow hobbyists. The island-style layout in the center of the room serves as an operating display, leaving the walls free for shelves. That's why many of the plans in this book are for island layouts. Because of space restrictions I haven't shown the entire room, but it should be easy enough to determine if one of these plans is suitable for the center of your train room. Another style of layout that has all but taken over scale model railroad design and seems to be increasingly popular with hi-railers is the walk-in or walkaround layout.

WALKAROUND DESIGN

Traditionally, toy train layouts are controlled using central control panels with one or more transformers, switches for powering a variety of blocks so two or more trains can be run at one time, and a control for each accessory on the layout. The owner stands at this panel and uses

Lionel's TrainMaster control system may be the most important development to hit the toy train hobby since the E-unit. The CAB-1 throttle has the potential to change the very nature of toy train layout design and construction by freeing us from centralized control panels.

this array of electrical devices to make magic happen on all parts of the railroad.

Years ago, scale train layouts were virtually identical, but in the last two decades a design called a "walkaround" layout has replaced all but the smallest island-style scale model railroads. The main line wraps its way around the room, with aisles alongside the path of the trains. Rather than standing back and surveying an entire miniature world as if they're looking down on the landscape from Mount Olympus, operators walk alongside their trains and get to see the world from the point of view of an engineer. Not only do they get a nice up-close view of the equipment, they also have the thrill of not knowing what lies beyond the next bend!

Walkaround design offers toy train operators several advantages in addition to simply getting a better look at the

trains as they wind their way throughout the countryside. First, in walkaround track plans, the track is much closer to the edge of the table than on a traditional toy train layout. As anyone who has ever spend an afternoon duck-walking across the top of a large flat tabletop layout can tell you, it's much more enjoyable to stand fully erect in an aisle to build or repair trackwork and scenery.

Another advantage to a walkaround layout, especially for toy train operators, is easy access to all those operating accessories that always seem to need a little extra help. Haven't you ever had to help those little cows get in or out of their stockcar, or adjust the operating milk car? It's a lot easier when you're only inches away from the accessory. No longer will visitors shake their heads as they watch you push buttons from across the road, only to have the fun turn into frustration as the milk cans refuse to fly out of that car one after the other.

Now that I've sold you on the advantages of a walkaround layout, you may be asking yourself why every other toy train operator hasn't chosen walkaround design. Well, the first reason probably has something to do with the wall displays mentioned earlier. These are traditional in the toy train world, and they lend themselves to island layouts in the center of the room. But if your main interest is operating and construction and not collecting, the main reason toy train layouts have lagged behind their scale modeling counterparts in adopting walkaround layout design has been a technological one—there simply wasn't a walkaround commercial control system available for AC powered toy trains. Walkaround control requires more than adding aisleways following the path of the main line, it also requires a handheld control unit so the operators can control the speed, direction, and routing of each train.

In late 1994, Lionel Trains Inc., in cooperation with Liontech, introduced a walkaround control system especially designed for toy trains. Called TrainMaster, the system replaced the large, heavy, traditional transformers like the ZW with a centralized power unit called a PowerHouse. This unit plugs into the wall and supplies constant AC voltage to a second unit called a PowerMaster. The PowerHouse unit provides power to the track. All train control functions are handled by means of a remote (wireless) handheld unit called a CAB-1. This looks like a television remote control with a large red speed control knob. As it is, the TrainMaster system can control one train. Dividing the layout into blocks (each with its own PowerHouse and PowerMaster) allows you to run as many trains as you can handle. It's easy to switch from one block to another using the CAB-1.

One disadvantage to using conventional block power control in conjunction with a walkaround-style track plan is that the block power controls seem never to be in the right place. Picture this—you're following your train around the layout and upon arriving at the next block, you turn the block power switch for your throttle. When you leave that block, you need to run back and throw the switch back so the next engineer doesn't loose control of his train when he enters the block you just left. Is there a way around that? Of course there is, and it's called command control.

COMMAND CONTROL

Since the very first model railroad, hobbyists have been trying to find a way to control trains just like the big boys—one engineer per train, operated and controlled completely independently of one another.

Command control is simple in theory and operation, but to understand how it works you need to understand how block, or cab control works. With traditional block control the layout is divided into any number of electrically isolated sections of track. Transformers put power on the rails, and each transformer will control any trains in that block. Put two or more locomotives in the block, all will run at the same relative speed and in the same direction. With block control you're not controlling the trains, you're actually controlling the direction and amount of current applied to the motors inside the locomotives.

With command control, all the track on the layout has a constant voltage. Why doesn't this voltage simply send trains racing around the main line with wild abandon? Each locomotive is equipped with a receiver located in the path of current between the track and the motor. The command control unit, called a command station, translates the control indications from the throttle into an electronic signal that tells the locomotive what to do. Each locomotive has its own unique signal, or "address." Suddenly, each engineer is controlling his (or her) own train completely independently of all the other trains on the layout.

If you have a very large layout you may need more than a single power station to keep a constant voltage on the track. These zones, which are each powered by an independent power unit, should be kept independent of other units to make any future troubleshooting easier. Also, if one power supply shorts out for any reason, having multiple power supplies means the entire layout won't shut down. Look at it this way: While you're crawling around under the layout trying to get things going again, at least *someone* can be having fun running trains!

The previous example may leave you thinking that command control is strictly for large, elaborate walkaround layouts. But command control is an ideal choice for small layouts where the trains are always close together. You don't have to worry about throwing block control switches every few seconds as the trains race their way around the main line.

Perhaps one of the biggest advantages to command control involves introducing the hobby to adults and children. Imagine you have some guests who aren't hobbyists but are quite fascinated by the layout in the basement. Naturally, you want to show off your masterpiece and ask your guests to run a train. But before they get started you have to explain a variety of switches, buttons, and dials. In many ways it's like sticking your head in the cockpit of a 737 and having the pilot asking you to take control! Typically, the guests will hang back and say "That's okay, I'll watch while you run the trains." Compare that with command control. You dial up the engine number, hand your guest the throttle and tell them to have fun. Simple and easy to use.

It should come as no surprise that Lionel has introduced a command station for the TrainMaster control station. Most of Lionel's new locomotives are equipped at the factory with a receiver. Receivers may also be available to equip your older Lionel models for command control. (The receiver doesn't affect control of the locomotive with conventional AC power.) Command control gives you freedom from throwing switches to control track power and lets you follow your train all around. Of course, with completely independent train control collisions become a real possibility.

In addition to controlling the speed and direction of travel, Lionel's command control system also lets engineers throw switches, operate horns and whistles, turn locomotive lights on and off, and even operate accessories—all using a handheld control unit. Don't worry about building a big control panel for your layout. With command control, they'll be a thing of the past.

ABOUT THIS BOOK

Each of the following chapters includes a track plan for an O gauge layout designed to depict the operating and visual characteristics of a particular prototype railroad. The track list shows the number and types of pieces of track and accessories shown on the plan. I've also listed some of the toy trains that are available in the particular prototype roadname featured in the plan. Of course, new products are coming out every day (or at least every week!), so check with your local hobby shop for the latest information.

The plans aren't arranged in any particular order, but I tried to include a representative sampling of well-known North American railroads. Space precludes including every possible railroad, and if I missed your favorite line, I'm sorry. But there's no reason the Illinois Central plan couldn't be used as is to depict the Santa Fe in Illinois, or the Seaboard Coast Line in Georgia. Most of the plans are fairly humble in size (no bigger than a two-car garage), but there are one or two dreamers in here. Let's get started—I hope you enjoy the journey. All Aboard!

Computer-Aided Design (CAD)

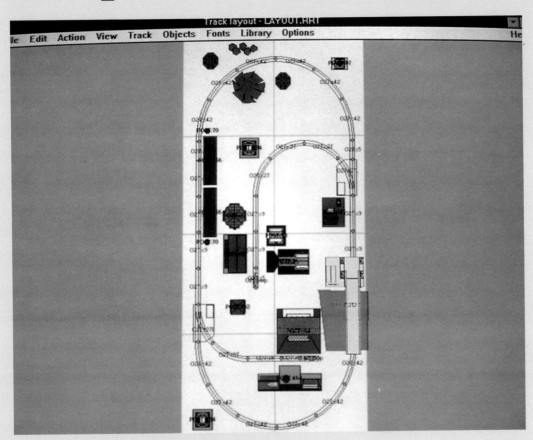

Although you can design a perfectly acceptable toy train layout using pencil and paper and a commercial template, more toy train operators are using home computers to design new or future layouts. Most layout designers at some point consider using a Computer-Aided Drafting, or CAD, program to design their layouts.

While CAD programs are perfectly fine for those who are familiar with them, I don't advise you to run out and buy CAD software if all you plan to do is design a layout with it. It's much easier, and far cheaper, to use a program specifically designed for toy trains. I've tried many of these programs, but the best one I can recommend is the one I used for this book: RR-Track version 2.4 by R&S Enterprises.

Although I like everything about this program, the best reason for toy train layout designers to use it is the extensive track and accessory libraries. Rather than trying to draw these elements yourself—which would be necessary with an ordinary CAD program—you can get them right out of the libraries.

RR-Track is a DOS-based program that requires Windows 3.1 operating system on a PC. After entering the overall dimensions of the room (which can be changed at any time), you select track from one of several libraries, including Lionel and Gar-Graves sectional track and switches, and switches from Ross Custom Switches and Curtis HiRail. (LGB large scale, American Flyer S gauge and even HO and N gauge sectional track libraries are also included.)

Other accessory libraries, as well as a custom-drawing feature for adding buildings and scenic elements to the plan are also included with this amazing software package.

Suppliers and Manufacturers

Arttista
1616 S. Franklin St.
Philadelphia, PA 19148
Handpainted action figures

Berkshire Valley Models
P. O. Box 150
Adams, MA 01220
Detail parts and buildings

Bowser Mfg. Co.
21 Howard St.
P. O. Box 322
Montoursville, PA 17754-0322
Handpainted figures, turntables

Buildings Unlimited
P. O. Box 239
Nazareth, PA 18064
Buildings, railroad structures

Circuitron/Scale Scenics
P. O. Box 322
Riverside, IL 60546,
Electronic products

Classic Toy Trains magazine
21027 Crossroads Circle
P. O. Box 1612
Waukesha, WI 53187
The leading magazine for toy train collectors and operators

CTT, Inc.
109 Medallion Center
Dallas, TX 75214
Track-design templates

Curtis Hi-Rail Products, Inc.
P. O. Box 385
North Stonington, CT 06359
Switches, track, and accessories

Dallee Electronics
10 Witmer Rd.
Lancaster, PA 17602
Electronic controllers, whistles

Depotronics, Inc.
P. O. Box 2093
Warrendale, PA 15086
Electronic controllers

Design Preservation Models
P. O. Box 66
Linn Creek, MO 65052,
Building kits

Dremel
4915 21st St.
Racine, WI 53406
Motor tools

GarGraves Trackage
Rt. 1, Box 255A
North Rose, NY 14516
Switches and track

Grandt Line Products
1040-B Shary Ct.
Concord, CA 94518
Switchstands, detail parts

Highball Products
P. O. Box 43633
Cincinnati, OH 45243
Track ballast

House of Balsa
10101 Yucca Rd.
Adelanto, CA 92301
Tuf-Grind

Kalmbach Publishing Co.
21027 Crossroads Circle
P. O. Box 1612
Waukesha, WI 53187
Model railroading books and magazines

K.B's Die-Cast Direct
1009 Twilight Trail
Frankfort, KY 40601
Automobiles, trucks, tractors

Keil Line Models
6440 McCullom Lake Rd.
Wonder Lake, IL 60097,
Signals, detail parts

K-Line Electric Trains
P. O. Box 2831
Chapel Hill, NC 27515
Locomotives, rolling stock, accessories

Lionel Corp.
50625 Richard W Blvd.
Chesterfield, MI 48051-2493
Locomotives, rolling stock, accessories

Mainline Modules
P. O. Box 21861
Chattanooga, TN 37421
Vinyl roadbed

MTH Electric Trains
9693-A Gerwig Lane
Columbia, MD 21046
Locomotives and rolling stock

Model Railroader magazine
21027 Crossroads Circle
P. O. Box 1612
Waukesha, WI 53187
Leading model railroad magazine, serving all scales

Moondog Express
104 W. Ocean Ave.
Lompoc, CA 93436
Rubber ties, streets, track patterns

N. J. International
77 W. Nicholai St.
Hicksville, NY 11801
Switch machines, signals

Oakridge Corporation
P. O. Box 247
Lemont, IL 60439
Model railroad supplies

Plastruct
1020 S. Wallace Pl.
City of Industry, CA 91748
Oil tanks, plastic structural details

R&S Enterprises
P. O. Box 643
Jonestown, PA 17038
Layout software

Red Caboose
P. O. Box 250
Mead, CO 80542
Locomotives

Ross Custom Switches
P. O. Box 110
North Stonington, CT 06359
Switches, track, and accessories

Stevens International
P. O. Box 126
Magnolia, NJ 08049
Animals, people

Sunset Models, Inc.
(Third Rail)
37 South 4th St.
Campbell, CA 95008
Locomotives, rolling stock

Wm. K. Walthers Inc.
P. O. Box 3039
Milwaukee, WI 53201-3039
Dwarf signals, railroad supplies

Weaver Models
div. Quality Craft Models Inc.
177 Wheatley Ave.
Northumberland, PA 17857
Rolling stock, locomotives

Williams Reproductions Ltd.
6660 Dobbin Rd.
Columbia, MD 21045
Locomotives and rolling stock

Woodland Scenics
P. O. Box 98
Linn Creek, MO 65052
Scenery materials

1 The Wild West

It's 1905 and Virginia & Truckee 4-4-0 no. 17, the *Columbus,* is rolling a V&T freight into Reno, Nevada. Just look at the polished boiler and brass trim! Those were the days when an engineer was assigned a steed and keeping it well-polished was a matter of pride. Stanley G. Palmer photo.

This is a nostalgic layout that will fit into just about any spare room, basement, garage, or attic. In this case, rather than cram all the items necessary to depict a modern railroad onto a 4 x 8 sheet of plywood, we've decided to let history be our friend and take advantage of the small size of the trains of the 1800s. At the same time, we'll do our best to capture the spirit and legend of the early wild west, with saloons, gunfights, lawmen, badmen, and just a plain old wild time. Luckily, we can leave out the gritty realities of the western expansion if we so choose. This is, after all, still a hobby.

The prototype railroad we've chosen to inspire our adventure is the Virginia & Truckee Railroad, which despite the name, was located nowhere near the Old Dominion state.

RAILS TO THE COMSTOCK

In the days of the 1849 California Gold Rush, Nevada was just a long, hot death trap to the would-be miners heading west to the Sacramento mountains. Little did those prospectors know their lust for gold had them walking right over the tremendous silver deposits in the Comstock Mountains in Nevada.

Here's another view of 4-4-0 no. 17 as it takes on water at Reno. The photo dates to 1900. Note the water tank that looks like a small building. It wouldn't be hard to build one for your V&T layout. Stanley G. Palmer photo.

Ironically, the miners discovered some gold in the area, but it took them a while to discover that the bluish rock they had to move out of the way to reach the gold deposits was actually silver ore. Needless to say, this error wasn't overlooked for long, and the Comstock region experienced a boom. Virginia City sprang up overnight and quickly became a real western town right out of the movies.

But a more efficient means was needed to move the silver ore out of the Comstock and to bring supplies into the mining camps and towns of the region. The Virginia & Truckee was that means, and the line was incorporated on March 5, 1868. Construction was completed to a connection with the Central (later Southern) Pacific on August 24, 1872.

The V&T made money from the start— no big trick when you serve what was the largest silver-producing area in the world. Like many western towns, Virginia City was leveled by fire in 1875. This only helped the V&T, since it added the materials needed to rebuild the city to its traffic base. But production in the mines, and the railroad's fortunes, began to decline, and the railroad, along with many of the towns

it served, was a mere shadow of its former glory days by the 1920s.

Interestingly, the V&T became something of an operating railroad museum in its later years, and many of the line's equipment and locomotives went on to starring roles in television shows and movies. The heritage of the V&T lives on today with a tourist railroad that operates a former V&T ten-wheeler in excursion service. But the glory days of Pullman sleepers and wild times on the Comstock are long gone.

THE SILVER CITY IN 36 SQUARE FEET

The track plan here includes enough accessories and operation to add interest to a fairly humble loop schematic. The coal loader can be easily adapted to become a silver ore loader. Only the finest mounts and draft horses are shipped into Virginia City and off-loaded at the corral from the V&T horse car.

A log unloader is used to unload the mining timbers needed to keep the tunnels from collapsing in on themselves. "Main Street" is nothing more than a wide dirt path that chokes the inhabitants with dust in the summer and bogs them down

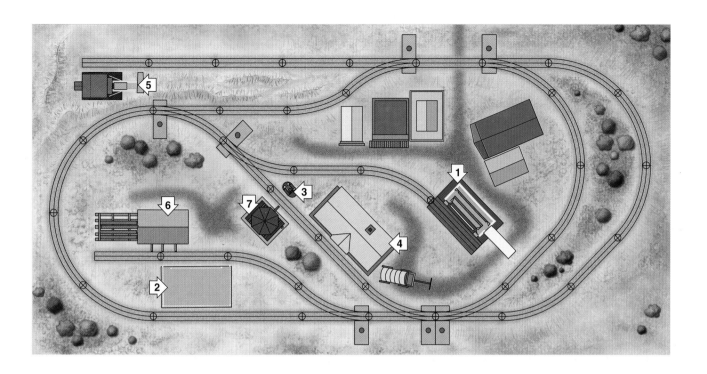

Frontier Trains

Locomotives
LION	1862	W&ARR General 4-4-0, green 1862 tender, 59–62
LION	18702	V&TRR, Steam, 4-4-0, "8702" on cab (SSS), 88
LION	1872	W&ARR General 4-4-0, 1872T/1875W with tender, 59–62
LION	1882	W&ARR General 4-4-0, 1882T tender, 60
LION	8630	W&ARR 4-4-0, General, 86
LION	8701	W&ARR General, yellow lettering, 77–79

Rolling Stock
LION	3370	W&ARR Sheriff and Outlaw Car, 61–64
LION	7312	W&ARR Stock Car, yellow lettering, 86
LION	9553	W&ARR Flatcar with fences, 6 horses, 78–80

Passenger Cars
LION	1865	W&ARR Coach, brown roof, 59–62
LION	1866	W&ARR Baggage, brown roof, 59–62
LION	1875	W&ARR Coach, Tuscan roof, 59–62
LION	1875W	W&ARR Coach, Tuscan roof, 59–62
LION	1876	W&ARR Baggage, Tuscan roof, 59–62
LION	1885	W&ARR Coach, brown roof, 60
LION	16010	V&TRR Passenger Car (SSS), 88
LION	16011	V&TRR Coach, yellow sides/gray roof (SSS), 88
LION	16012	V&TRR Baggage car (SSS), 88

Wild West Track

Track
Lionel O31 Curve 45° (12)
Lionel O31 Modern Right-Hand Turnout (4)
Lionel Single Straight (14)
Lionel O31 Modern Left-Hand Turnout (3)
Lionel Custom-Cut Straight (1)
Lionel Cut Stock Curve (1)

Structures
1 Lionel 3656 Stockyard (1)
2 Lionel 3356 Horse Car Platform (1)
3 Lionel 151 Semaphore Signal (1)
4 Lionel/MPC 2783 Freight Station (1)
5 Lionel 12712 Ore Loader (1)
6 Lionel 12774 Lumber Loader (1)
7 Lionel 12711 Water Tower (1)

in muck in the winter, but it features all the, ah, pleasures of home. (You're on your own for that, but certainly a saloon, dance hall, and jail for the miscreants seem the minimum requirements.)

I've also added a station and an operating water tank to the center of town, but you may want to consider building a model of one the V&T's unique water tanks to really add some character to the layout.

The 1800s aren't popular with train manufacturers right now, but that doesn't mean you won't have any equipment to run on the layout. Lionel's General is not a true

The Virginia & Truckee was truly a railroad where time stood still. This photo in Gold Hill, Nevada, dates to 1938 (note the pickup truck) but the railroad is still firmly locked in the 1890s. H. Sullivan photo.

V&T locomotive, but it does capture the looks of the western line's extensive fleet of 4-4-0s. Add an assortment of old-time passenger and freight cars, and you have the makings of an interesting roster that won't drain your wallet or leave the layout so full of equipment that nothing can move.

Remember, just because you don't have a large area for a layout doesn't mean you can't build a layout that reflects the real world. Sometimes you just have to turn back the clock and find a smaller prototype.

Transporting perishables to the north was an important part of the FEC's business. Here one of the road's unusual BL2s switches a produce warehouse. Harry M. Wolfe photo.

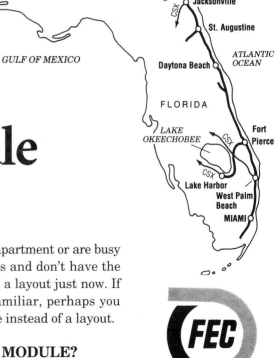

2 An FEC Module
A small slice of Florida

Perhaps you want to get into railroading with toy trains, but aren't ready to dedicate the entire basement, garage, or attic—and a fair portion of your spare time—without sampling the waters first. Or maybe you want to try hi-railing, but you're not yet ready to tear down your traditional Lionel Lines layout to make way for the Semi-scale Central. Or maybe you live in an apartment or are busy with other obligations and don't have the space or time to build a layout just now. If any of this sounds familiar, perhaps you should build a module instead of a layout.

WHAT IS A MODULE?

As the name implies, a module is a section of layout that is interchangeable

Florida East Coast Track

Track
Curtis HiRail Straight, 14.5 in. (3)
Curtis HiRail/GarGraves Straight, 37.25 in. (1)
Curtis Excel no. 6 Turnout, Left-Hand (3)
Curtis HiRail/GarGraves Cut Straight (9)
Curtis HiRail Turnout Transition Curve (3)
Curtis Excel no. 6 Turnout, Right-Hand (2)

Structures
 1 Lionel 12734 Passenger/Freight Station (1)
 2 Lionel 12761 Animated Billboard (1)
 3 Lionel 12733 Watchman's Shanty (1)
 4 Lionel 12722 Roadside Diner (1)
 5 Lionel 12730 Girder Bridge (2)
 6 Lionel 6-2162 Crossing Gate w/signal (2)
 7 Lionel 12773 Freight Platform (1)
 8 Lionel 12704 Dwarf Block Signal (2)
 9 Lionel 2127 Diesel Horn Shed (1)
10 Lionel 12884 Truck Loading Dock (1)

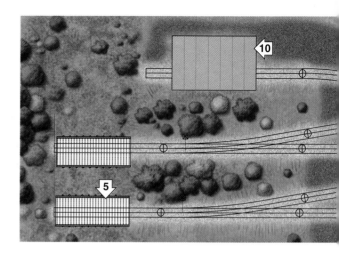

The Florida East Coast was one of those railroads that couldn't resist choosing a brilliant paint scheme for its diesel locomotives. Red, orange, and silver F7 no. 508 shows off the FEC's original scheme. William F. Husa, Jr. photo.

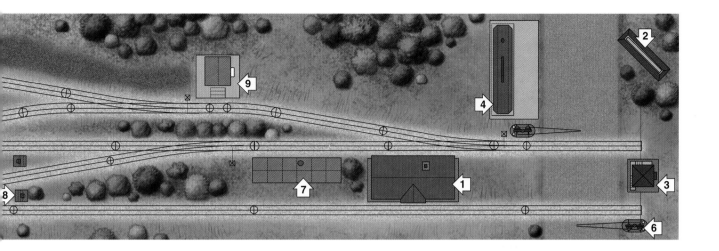

with other modules. Modular layouts got started in the United States with the Ntrak movement (an organization of N scale modelers) in the early 1970s, and today modelers in every major gauge and scale, and some minor ones, have a set of modular standards.

Here's how it works: Each modeler builds his or her own module. Since things like the distance of track centers from the edge of the module, height above the floor, and wiring are built according to predetermined specifications, all modules are completely interchangeable.

Although many module clubs have work nights when members help each other with modules, the fun really comes when the group sets up the entire layout for a train show. If you've never seen it before, it's amazing to watch—everyone brings in their modules and in a few hours' time a number of layouts in all the major scales are up and running. Since modular railroading is a social activity by definition, it lets you get out of the basement and have a good time with people who share the same interest. And since modules by definition are small, they don't take a lifetime to finish. You could easily be up and running and ready to hit the road with only a few weekends' worth of work.

Florida East Coast Trains

Diesel Engines
LION 8064	FEC GP-9 Powered, silver trucks, 80	
LION 8065	FEC GP-9 Dummy, silver trucks, 80	
MTH 2007	FEC F-3 AA Units (O27), 97	
MTH 2012	FEC F-3 B Unit (O27), 97	
MTH 2052	FEC F-3 AA Units, 95	
MTH 2060	FEC F-3 B Unit, 95	
MTH 2130	FEC BL-2, 96	

Rolling Stock
LION 9443	FEC Boxcar, silver roof and ends, 81	
LION 9443	Southern TCA FEC Boxcar, 81	
LION 19209	FEC Boxcar, dark blue, 88	
LION 9382	FEC Caboose, silver stripe, 80	
LION 6200	FEC Gondola w/ canisters, yellow letters, 81–82	

Passenger Cars
MTH 6005	FEC 60' Streamlined Passenger Cars, set of 5, 94–95	
MTH 6040	FEC Streamlined Passenger Cars, set of 4 (O27), 97	
MTH 6105	FEC 60' Streamlined Passenger Car set of 2, 96	

STANDARDS

Although O gauge modules are commonplace, it's a good idea to contact a local club and find out what their specific requirements are before you spend time building a module only to find out the local group requires 6-inch track centers instead of the 5½-inch centers you used.

Typically modules are built in 4-foot lengths, with a standard width of 2 feet, although optional widths of as much as 36 inches are permitted. The module shown

The lack of dynamic brakes on these GP7s indicate just how flat the territory served by the Florida East Coast is. That flat terrain makes it an ideal choice as a theme for an O gauge module. Scotty Laird photo.

here is really three modules together for a total length of 12 feet. (It could also be two 6-footers, but just make sure you can get the modules to and from the show site. Cars are getting smaller and smaller, and model railroads don't travel well in the rear of vehicles like pickup trucks.)

The prototype inspiration for our modules comes from the Florida East Coast, a small railroad with a fascinating history that includes deadly violence resulting from labor strikes and hurricanes. On the positive side, FEC operated some very colorful locomotives, and toy train manufacturers have produced several of them. Also, as a subsidiary of Atlantic Coast Line for many years, FEC played host to some of the ACL's more colorful purple and silver trains—certainly an attention-getting roster for a small layout designed to go to public showings.

I've included a produce loading dock and a small station on the plan and have also decided to use Ross Custom track. After all, it's only a small module, so why not

make this foray into hi-railing look as good as possible? One note—many modular clubs insist on using Lionel O gauge track so postwar equipment can run without any of the operational problems some older trains experience when operating through the frogs of custom switches.

The selection of the east coast of Florida offers another advantage that may not seem obvious until the first time you try to cram these modules into a small car. Florida scenery is flat, very flat. Not having to allow for mountains on a module is a real plus. Here we've chosen a theme that works with us and not against us.

Finally, consider using less traditional construction methods for building a module. Remember, every pound you add to the module is another pound you'll be carrying around. Modular railroading offers a great way to get out of the armchair and into the active side of the hobby. So even if you don't have room for a layout, go ahead and see if a module fits in your life—you'll be glad you did.

Unless you've seen them, it's hard to imagine just how tall grain elevators can be. No granger road would be complete with them. Silos like these could be modeled from PVC pipe or cardboard mailing tubes. Stan Miller photo.

3 Chicago & North Western Prairie Line

The Chicago & North Western strikes north from the rail hub of Chicago into the iron ore regions of Michigan's Upper Peninsula and as far west as the plains states of Nebraska and South Dakota.

The C&NW can trace its ancestry back to 1859. While the line expanded into Wisconsin with the acquisition of the Chicago & Milwaukee in 1866, the most notable railroad acquired by the C&NW was the Omaha Road—the Chicago, St. Paul, Minneapolis & Omaha RR—which maintained a separate corporate existence until 1972.

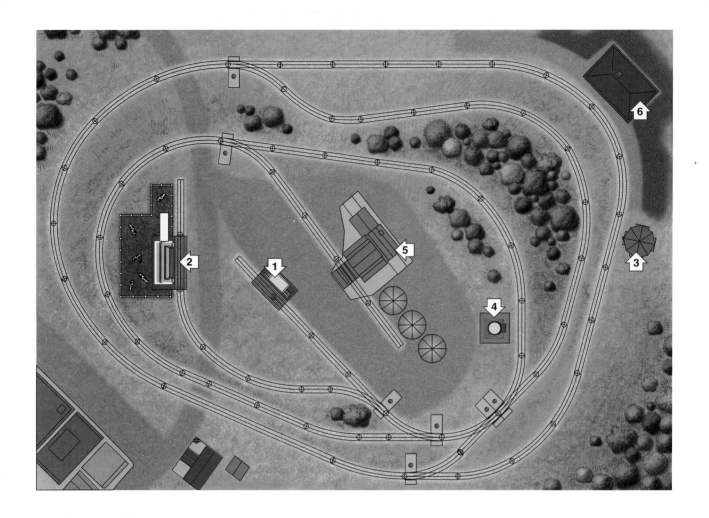

Chicago & North Western Track

Track
Lionel O31 Modern Left-Hand Turnout (3)
Lionel O42 Curve 30° (12)
Lionel O54 Curve (16)
Lionel Single Straight (24)
Lionel O31 Modern Right-Hand Turnout (4)
Lionel O72 Curve 22.5° (5)
Lionel Custom-Cut Straight (2)
Lionel Cut Stock Curve (1)
Lionel Half Straight (3)
Lionel O31 Curve 45° (1)

Structures
1 Lionel 3462P Milk Car Platform (1)
2 Lionel 3656 Stock Yard (1)
3 Lionel 30 Water Tower (1)
4 Lionel 193 Industrial Water Tower (1)
5 Lionel 12726 Grain Elevator (1)
6 Lionel 12812 Illuminated Freight Station (1)

The Planters sign makes a great decoration and advertisement on the side of a grain elevator in Clinton, Iowa, as the C&NW's Train no. 2, once known as the *Kate Shelley,* departs behind a single E7A. Phil Hastings photo.

The North Western also experienced a significant expansion with the acquisition of the Chicago Rock Island & Pacific's Minneapolis–Kansas City route when the Rock disappeared in 1980.

Chicago & North Western, under the auspices of subsidiary Western Railroad Properties, extended its main line south into the Powder River basin of Wyoming to serve the extensive coal fields in that region. (This line is jointly operated with the Burlington Northern.)

Like most contemporary railroads, C&NW has spun off some of its lines to form smaller regional railroads. These include the Dakota, Minnesota & Eastern in September 1986 and the Fox River Valley Railroad in Wisconsin in 1988. This isolated the C&NW Upper Peninsula lines, which carry lots of iron ore tonnage, from the remainder of the North Western system. Ore trains do operate over the Fox River via a trackage rights agreement.

In 1995 Union Pacific purchased the Chicago & North Western. Almost overnight, equipment and operations began to reflect the line's inclusion in the far-flung UP empire. But that doesn't mean

Chicago & North Western Trains

Steam Engines

LION	18612	C&NW 2-6-4 "8612", 89
MTH	1112	C&NW USRA 0-8-0 (O27), 96
WVR	1019	C&NW 0-6-0 Switcher, 92
WMS	5008	C&NW USRA 4-6-2 Pacific, 89

Diesel Engines

LION	8056	C&NW Trainmaster, 80
LION	8776	C&NW GP-20 Powered, 77–78
LION	18219	C&NW Dash 8-40C "8501", black roof/rails, 95
LION	18816	C&NW GP-38-2 Diesel "4600", 92
MTH	2006	C&NW SD-60 (O27), 96
MTH	2035	C&NW GP-9, green, 94
MTH	2078	C&NW H10-44, 95
MTH	2136	C&NW AS-616, 96
ROW	5540	C&NW FT AB Units, N/A
ROW	554046	C&NW FT AB Units, N/A
3RD	No Number	C&NW Dash C44-9W, 96
WVR	1313	C&NW Alco C-628, 94
WVR	5517	C&NW RS-3 "1624", 90
WVR	No Number	C&NW Alco FA-2 Unit, 90
WVR	No Number	C&NW Alco FB-2 Unit, 90
WMS	F7201	C&NW F-7 ABA Units, 95

Rolling Stock

LION	16617	C&NW Boxcar w/ end-of-train device, 89
WMS	FC22	C&NW Boxcar, green, 93–95
LION	9361	C&NW Bay Window Caboose, green roof, 80
LION	16533	C&NW Bay Window Caboose, yellow ladders, 92
MTH	7707	C&NW Caboose, 96
LION	16121	C&NW Stock Car (SSS), 92
MTH	7109	C&NW Stock Car, 96
LION	16334	C&NW TTUX Flatcar set w/ trailers "16337", 91
ROW	314035	C&NW Flatcars w/ Ertl Tractors, 94
MTH	7205	C&NW Gondola w/ crates, 96
LION	6135	C&NW ACF Hopper, black/yellow lettering, 86
LION	19322	C&NW Ore Car w/ load, 93
LION	19502	C&NW Refrigerator, green and yellow, 87
MTH	9403	C&NW Reefer, 96
MTH	9203	C&NW Tank Car, 96
WMS	M209	C&NW Madison Passenger set, yellow/green, 95

The Chicago & North Western operated numerous lines through the small farm towns of the upper Midwest—scenes and places that provide lots of inspiration for a model railroad layout. Randolph, Minnesota, is one of those places. Mike Schafer photo.

the C&NW can't live on in your very own model empire.

PRAIRIE REGION C&NW LAYOUT

The 7 x 10-foot island layout, while not huge by any standards, will let you capture the scenery and operations of the C&NW's far-flung granger lines in North Dakota, Minnesota, or Wisconsin. The track plan consists of two ovals, one inside the other and connected at a small junction. That means you can run two trains at once on the layout or, more important, run one longer train through both ovals. This will lengthen the apparent mainline run and let you operate trains that don't look as if they're merely chasing their tails around the layout.

Grain traffic is the backbone of rail lines through the upper Midwest, so the centerpiece of the layout, quite literally, is the Lionel grain elevator kit. You can make the facility even more imposing by adding

a number of metal grain storage bins alongside. Since this is farm country, we've also included a milk car unloading platform (Wisconsin is the dairy state!) and a cattle loader. A small station and a water tank for the steam era (board up the station and scrap the tank for a more contemporary look), as well as a Main Street scene of general store, gas station, and a few houses give the builder a place where he or she can spend many pleasant evenings adding details.

Although there aren't thousands of examples of C&NW lettered equipment available, a fair number have come along over the years. Since the layout is so small, perhaps you could acquire some used equipment and paint and reletter it for the North Western.

Can't have an interesting O gauge layout in 7 x 10 feet? Nonsense, the C&NW Prairie Line offers interesting operation, multitrain hands-off running, and a chance to really detail a small town scene.

Illinois Central is a north-south railroad in a world of east-west trunk lines. The main line links Chicago with New Orleans. IC's passenger equipment wore a handsome orange and chocolate brown paint scheme during the postwar era. Here, Train no. 6, the *Panama Limited,* departs Union Station, New Orleans, bound for Chicago. Elliott Kahn photo.

4 The Illinois Central RR
More than just a song

The Illinois Central Railroad is not only one of the oldest lines in the United States, it's also one of the best known. The popular song "City of New Orleans" laments the sad state of railroad passenger travel in the mid and late 1960s. But that was a long time ago, and now the Illinois Central, a much leaner route shed of much duplicate mileage, remains a critical part of the Midwestern rail network.

The IC has a rich and lengthy history, counting among its ranks of former employees both Abraham Lincoln, who was a railroad lawyer before fate intervened, and Samuel Langhorne Clemens, also known as Mark Twain.

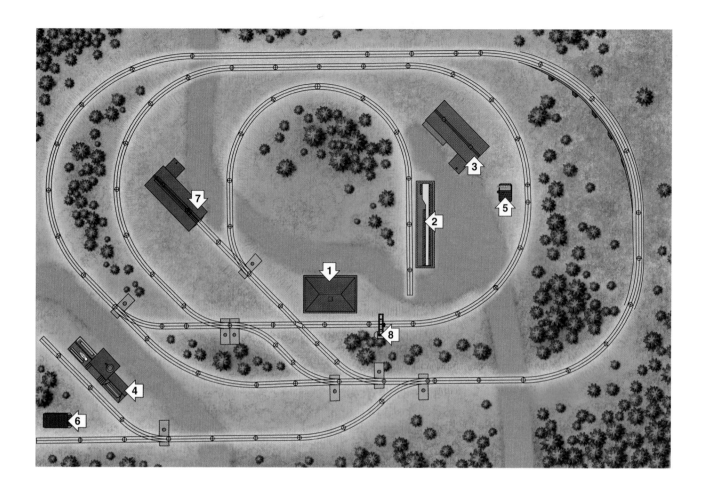

Illinois Central Track

Track
Lionel O72 Curve 22.5° (8)
Lionel O54 Curve (24)
Lionel O31 Modern Left-Hand Turnout (2)
Lionel Single Straight (25)
Lionel Half Straight (6)
Lionel 40-in Straight (1)
Lionel O31 Modern Right-Hand Turnout (6)
Lionel 45° Cross (1)
Lionel O42 Curve 30° (6)
Lionel Custom-Cut Straight (3)
Lionel Uncoupling Track (1)

Structures
1 Lionel 133 Passenger Station (1)
2 Lionel 362 Barrel Loader (1)
3 Lionel 12905 Factory (1)
4 Lionel 12873 Operating Sawmill (1)
5 Lionel 12718 Barrel Shed (1)
6 Lionel 12705 Lumber Shed (1)
7 Lionel 12906 Maintenance Shed (1)
8 Lionel 12763 Single Gantry Signal (1)

WESTWA— OOPS, SOUTHWARD HO!

Unlike every other railroad of its time, the Illinois Central made its goal not California but the Gulf of Mexico and New Orleans. The Illinois Central achieved its goal by 1882. Then, over the next 20 years, the IC extended its routes by means of acquisition and expansion as far west as Omaha, Nebraska, and as far east as Birmingham, Alabama, and Indianapolis, Indiana. But the north-south corridor running roughly parallel to the mighty river was always the railroad's heart.

Honest Abe and Mark Twain weren't the only famous Americans connected with the IC. In 1900, near Meridian, Mississippi, an engineer named James Luther Jones perished in a relatively minor train wreck. An engine wiper named Wallace Saunders wrote a song about the "brave engineer" and the legend of "Casey" Jones was born.

In 1972 the IC merged with the Gulf, Mobile & Ohio to form the Illinois Central Gulf. ICG units received a fairly colorful (for the time) orange and white paint scheme. In recent years, the ICG has reformed itself as the Illinois Central, returned to a more conservative black paint scheme, and spun off many duplicate route miles to various new shortlines and regionals.

PLYWOOD PRAIRIES

The heart of the IC always was the fertile lands of central Illinois. Flat running and numerous crossings at grade with east-west railroads are important elements to capture the feel of the Midwest.

Large grain elevators, each one a little different, also earmark the right-of-way. To those not familiar with them, the first sight of these structures leaves little doubt where they got their nickname—

prairie skyscrapers. But the 8 x 12-foot island-style layout shown here depicts the IC farther south, in the pine woods of Mississippi.

We have a grade crossing, complete with a small station. The track crossing at grade can be ballasted and painted and weathered to look like a different railroad, certainly more grandiose than the switching lead it actually is.

A barrel loader, attached to a Lionel factory kit, serves as the main industry in town. Perhaps it's a ginseed oil (made from ginseed plants) factory, or perhaps you can declare it to be a distillery. A lumber loader in the center of the layout and a sawmill in one corner, separated by only a few feet, can be miles apart in the imagination. The rest of the layout is fairly open and scenic. The low ridge that runs from one corner to the other helps break up the round-and-round look without adding tall

In the heart of the Mississippi pine forest country, the railroad has to use lots of low pile trestles to keep the track above water. Adding these to a layout would be an interesting project that would really help set the scene. J. P. Lamb, Jr., photo.

Illinois Central Trains

Steam Engines
LION 18620	IC Steam, 2-6-2, yellow letters, 91
LION 18625	IC 4-4-2 "8625", 91

Diesel Engines
LION 2363	IC F-3 AB, orange stripe, 55–56
	(A) Black lettering
	(B) Brown lettering
LION 8030	IC GP-9 Powered, 70–72
LION 8580/8582	IC F-3 AA, orange/yellow stripe, 85–87
LION 8581	IC F-3 B Unit w/ horn, orange/yellow stripe, 85–87
LION 8669	IC U36B Powered, black lettering, 76–77
LION 18210	IC SD-40 "6006", 93
LION 18924	IC Industrial Diesel Switcher "8924", 94–95
RED RC-51	IC GP-9, 94

Rolling Stock
LION 1988	Midwest TCA IC Boxcar, 88
LION 6232	IC Boxcar (Std O), 86
LION 9200	IC Boxcar, black/white letters, 70-71
MTH 7404	IC Boxcar, 95
LION 9160	IC N5C Caboose, black/white lettering, 70-72
	(A) Regular production
	(B) With large "ITT" sticker
LION 19716	IC E/V Caboose w/ Smoke, 93
LION 9340	IC Gondola (O27), 79–83
	(A) Orange, black lettering, canisters
	(B) Red, white lettering, no canisters
LION 6113	IC Short Hopper, 83–85
LION 16042	IC Baggage, 2400-style brown body (O27), 91
LION 16043	IC Combine, brown body, orange stripe (O27), 91
LION 16044	IC Coach, brown body/orange stripe (O27), 91
LION 16045	IC Vista Dome, brown body (O27), 91
LION 16046	IC Coach, brown body/orange stripe (O27), 91
LION 16047	IC Observation, brown body (O27), 91
LION 16049	IC Diner, brown body (O27), 92
LION 16093	IC Full Vista Dome Car (O27), 95
LION 19129	IC Full Vista Dome Car, 93
WMS M214	IC Madison Passenger set, brown/orange, 94–95

Illinois Central, along with the Gulf, Mobile & Ohio, disappeared into the Illinois Central Gulf, adding yet more variety to the equipment you can run on an IC/ICG layout. Louis Saillard photo.

mountains that would look out of place in a south-central setting. Finally, a long, low trestle provides the railroad a crossing over a marshy plain and provides a great place to look at your trains as they wind their way around the layout. All this proves that a toy train layout doesn't have to overloaded with accessories to be interesting to view or operate.

Illinois Central and corporate successor Illinois Central Gulf had some interesting and colorful paint schemes and some that, while not exactly colorful, were certainly classy. You can use a black Red Caboose GP9 to pull the freights, and assign the Lionel IC F3 to the point of the handsome chocolate brown and orange *City of New Orleans*. I can almost hear the music playing in the background.

5 Engine Terminal
Got more locomotives than freight cars?

If you're like most toy train operators, you probably gravitate towards the locomotives every time you enter the local train store. You can't leave that store without at least one new engine every time the budget, or spouse, allows. And now you find yourself ready to build a model layout to proudly display these hard-earned trophies in a realistic and interesting setting—only to find you have 20 steam engines, 40 diesels, and a half dozen electrics. And all you have to put behind this massive fleet is a collection of ten assorted freight cars. You're obviously suffering from an extreme case of locomotive-itis.

You could sell some of your prized iron steeds and use those funds to acquire more rolling stock—but maybe you can have your cake and eat it too by creating a model railroad layout that makes the locomotives the center of attention. How? It's simple. Model an engine-servicing facility.

THE PROTOTYPE—
CENTERPIECE OF THE YARD

Prototype railroads maintain engine-servicing facilities at virtually every major junction with another railroad. These operations range from very basic—simple affairs with a single spur track and a way to get fuel and sand into the engine—to elaborate facilities with back-shops capable of rebuilding entire fleets of locomotives. All have one thing in

Engine Terminal Track

Track
Lionel O72 Curve 22.5° (24)
Lionel Single Straight (40)
Lionel O72 Left-Hand Turnout (12)
Lionel Half Straight (5)
Lionel 40-in. Straight (3)
Lionel Custom-Cut Straight (13)
Lionel O72 Right-Hand Turnout (2)
Lionel O54 Curve (4)

Structures
1 Lionel 350 Engine Transfer Table (1)
2 Lionel 350-50 Transfer Table Extension (1)
3 Lionel 195 Floodlight Tower (1)
4 Lionel 415 Diesel Fuel Station (1)
5 Lionel 138 Water Tower (1)
6 Lionel 182 Magnet Crane (1)
7 Lionel 497 Coaling Station (1)
8 Lionel 12767 Wheel Grind Module (1)
9 Lionel 12767 Steam Clean Module (1)
10 Lionel 12767 Train Wash Module (1)
11 Lionel 12897 Engine House (1)
12 Lionel 2302 UP Gantry Crane (1)
13 Lionel 12886 Floodlight Tower (1)
14 Lionel 12878 Illuminated Control Tower (1)

Some terminals have open-air engine houses like the UP's facility in East Los Angeles. Note the long inspection pit between the rails and the assortment of danger signs. Be sure to include these details on your model. Gordon Odegard photo.

common—the locomotives are always the center of attention.

While modern facilities are quite interesting, in the days when steam and diesel locomotives shared the rails the engine terminal was a beehive of activity. Within the confines of the terminal would be found coaling, watering, and sanding facilities for the steamers, a turntable or wye to turn the locomotives around, and ash-pits to remove the coal residue from the firebox. For the diesel locomotives there were wash racks, facilities for sanding and refueling. Occasionally the diesels would also get a ride on the turntable, but since most diesels are arranged in semipermanently coupled sets that can be easily controlled from either end, they don't require a turntable—one of the reasons these symbols of the steam era are pretty rare.

Refueling, cleaning, and minor repairs to prepare a locomotive for another run are referred to as "turning" the engine. (Note that "turning" may or may not actually involve spinning the engine around on a turntable or wye.) Major problems discovered when the locomotive was inspected, or periodic maintenance, would require a trip to the backshop. Backshops varied in their makeup and appearance,

but the purpose was always the same—get the locomotives fixed, and get them back on the road.

Locomotives represent a tremendous capital investment for any prototype (or model) railroad, and they don't make one penny for their owner by sitting idle, awaiting attention. For that reason most backshops were indoors, so repairs could be performed in all weather, and had a number of tracks parallel to one another. Large overhead gantry cranes literally picked up locomotives and moved them from one part of the shop to another. The tracks were straight, not arranged in a radial pattern as in a roundhouse, so workers had sufficient room to work at both the front and back of the locomotive. Transfer tables saved space and made it easy to move engines into and out of servicing tracks.

Steam locomotives had their tubes and fireboxes inspected and repaired. Usually air pumps, generators, and other auxiliary components would be removed and replaced with rebuilt items. This minimized the time the engine spent in the backshop, but it also meant that every time an engine was shopped its appearance might change considerably. These

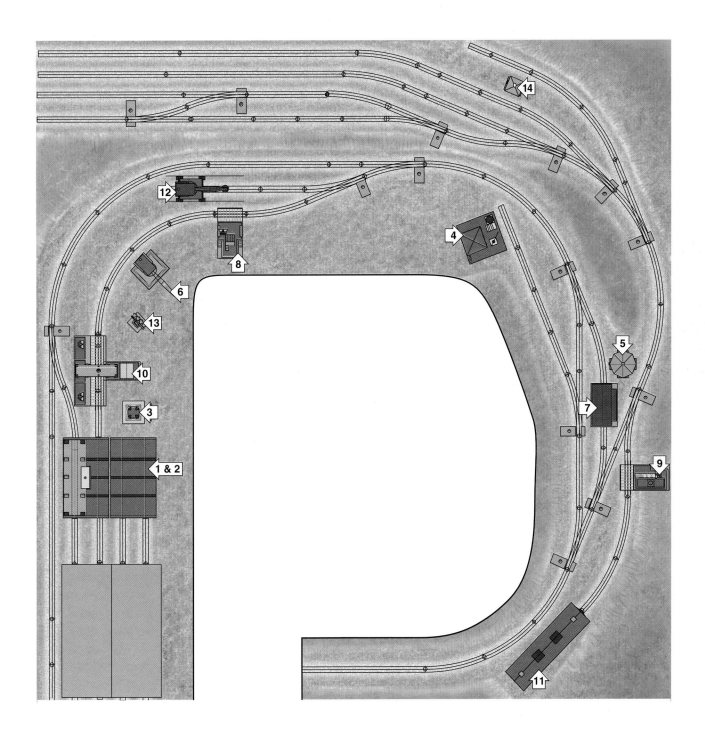

detail changes drive scale model railroaders nuts on occasion!

Most diesels have their wheels replaced or reground until the wheels are perfectly round. Diesels need a lot less frequent maintenance than steamers (the main reason railroads converted to diesel power was this maintenance savings), but they still require inspection of their cylinders and pistons for excessive wear. Their fuel tanks are emptied, cleaned, and in-

spected. Finally, both steam and diesel engines get a fresh coat of primer and paint. Then the locomotives are ready to be returned to service.

MODELING AN ENGINE-SERVICING FACILITY

The track plan shows a 12 x 12-foot layout that features O72 curves and switches so it can accommodate the largest three-rail locomotives. This isn't a layout for the

operator who wants to watch trains snake their way through the countryside, but it is one way to feature all those locomotives you've acquired over the years without needing a warehouse to house the railroad. Of course, if you have that warehouse, you can simply use this plan as an engine terminal and fill the rest of the room with mainline running.

The only way to fit this much railroad in such a small room and still allow a couple of operators to fit in with it is to use a point-to-point schematic. Locomotives await their turn to be serviced in one of five holding tracks located "offstage." While these tracks aren't hidden from view, I've shown them disguised behind building flats so they are as unobtrusive as possible.

Once the locomotive comes onto the scene you can route it to one of the many operating accessories that are included to depict the functions of a prototype engine terminal. I've included a wheel grinder, diesel wash rack, a fueling facility, and a transfer table. The gantry cranes are also quite practical for all those heavy lifting jobs in and around the terminal area. You can build large enginehouse or backshop structures using commercially available kits (Lionel or Korber), or check your hobby shop for some components to scratchbuild your own. The Kalmbach publication *Realistic Plastic Structures for Toy Train Layouts* offers plenty of helpful techniques for scratchbuilding. You can make the building as simple or complex as you'd like, but just be sure to include some big windows and maybe some interior details. The backshop is located right next to the door, and your visitors won't be able to resist the temptation to have a look inside.

Although this plan lacks continuous-running capability, it does provide a realistic setting for moving locomotives around as they prepare for their next run. A road engineer may not be pleased with the finished layout, but I can't think of a better cure for locomotive-itis!

Military trains sets, like the recent Lionel Navy and Coast Guard sets, have always been popular with collectors, operators, and even first-time set buyers. Why not display these trains at their best with a layout dedicated to Lionel's armed forces? Jim Forbes photos.

6 Military Railroad
An ideal way to display those action accessories

Toy manufacturers have always capitalized on the obsession young boys have with things military. Even today, many kids' playsets and action figures reflect some form of military organization, although the soldiers may be the loyal servants of the Queen of Zaldar or some other farfetched fantasy character.

Scale modelers, and many serious toy train operators, scoff at Lionel's extensive line of military action accessories. Train sets and add-on accessories have been designed featuring every branch of the service—Army, Navy, Air Force, and even the Coast Guard. The sheer multitude of military accessories makes it easy to create an entire layout dedicated to displaying these military sets and add-ons in the best

Military Trains

Diesel Engines

LION 18840   U.S. Army GP-7 "1821", white frame, 95
LION 18927   U.S. Navy NW-2 "65-00637", yellow, 94–95
LION 18938   U.S. Navy NW-2 Calf, black frame, 95
LION 8485   USMC NW-2 Switcher, camouflage, 84–85

Motorized Units

LION 41   U.S. Army Switcher, black, white lettering, 55–57
LION 51   U.S. Navy Yard Switcher, white lettering, 56–57
LION 59   Minuteman Switcher, red and blue letters, 62–63

Rolling Stock

LION 16566   U.S. Army SP-Type Caboose "907", 95
LION 16908   U.S. Navy Flatcar w/ black "930" submarine, 94–95
LION 16939   U.S. Navy Flatcar w/ orange boat "04040", 95
LION 3820   Flatcar w/ gray submarine, 60–62
LION 6640   USMC Rocket Launcher, 60
LION 6651   USMC Cannon Car, 64
LION 5727   USMC Bunk Car, 84–85
LION 16710   U.S. Army Operating Missile Car, red missile, 95
LION 19824   U.S. Army Target Launcher, w/small balloon, 96
LION 16116   U.S. Army Tank Car, 1-D, 91

Military Track

Track

Lionel O54 Curve (38)
Lionel Single Straight (41)
Lionel O31 Modern Right-Hand Turnout (4)
Lionel O31 Modern Left-Hand Turnout (4)
Lionel O31 Curve 45° (8)
Lionel Half Straight (3)
Lionel Custom-Cut Straight (4)

Structures

1 Lionel 175 Rocket Launcher (1)
2 Lionel 313 Bascule Bridge (1)
3 Lionel 282 Gantry Crane (1)
4 Lionel 943 Exploding Ammo Dump (4)
5 Lionel 419 Heliport Control Tower (1)
6 Lionel 462 Derrick Platform (1)
7 Lionel 192 Control Tower (1)
8 Lionel 193 Industrial Water Tower (1)
9 Lionel 470 Missile Launching Platform (1)
10 Lionel 2199 Microwave Tower (1)
11 Lionel 12749 Rotary Radar Antenna (1)
12 Lionel 12898 Flagpole (1)
13 Lionel 12884 Truck Loading Dock (1)
14 Lionel 12733 Watchman's Shanty (1)

possible light. It's a pity no real trains look like the military toy trains. Or do they?

PROTOTYPES FOR G.I. RAILROADS

You may be surprised to learn that military trains have operated since the American Civil War. In fact, that conflict is considered by many historians to be the first "railroad" war, and therefore the first modern war. Battles were fought and entire campaigns hinged on the control of rail junctions. Civil War engineers mounted huge siege guns and mortars on flatcars so they could be easily moved into firing position and transported to another location before the enemy could locate and silence them.

The use of railroads in warfare continued into the twentieth century. The Germans used large railroad-mounted guns in both World Wars. The U.S. Army Corps of Engineers includes a Transportation Corps that trained in the operation of all types of rail equipment, including steam locomotives, until only recently. And all the services, but especially the Navy, use small switching railroads to transport material from one area of a base to another.

But is there a basis in reality for the Lionel rolling stock? The searchlight car looks an awful lot like the cars used in many railroad wreck trains, or mounted in the cars Canadian National built during World War II to provide air defense for convoy loading ports on the coast.

Don't think there's a prototype for the Lionel missile firing car? Think again. During the Cold War the Air Force constructed several jumbo-sized freight cars that theoretically could be moved around the country at random in the event of a threat. These cars would be harder to knock out of action than a permanent missile base. The Air Force brass didn't take into account how easy these cars were for railfans to spot, and they never had much luck keeping the missile moves a secret.

With all these prototype examples, why not build a military layout? It's sure to be popular, since—let's face it—the military operating accessories are by far the most fun!

THE TRACK PLAN

The layout plan is a fairly simple water-wing-style continuous-run loop. It features a base that includes a small harbor equipped with a pier and crane to handle the operating submarine, a heliport, and

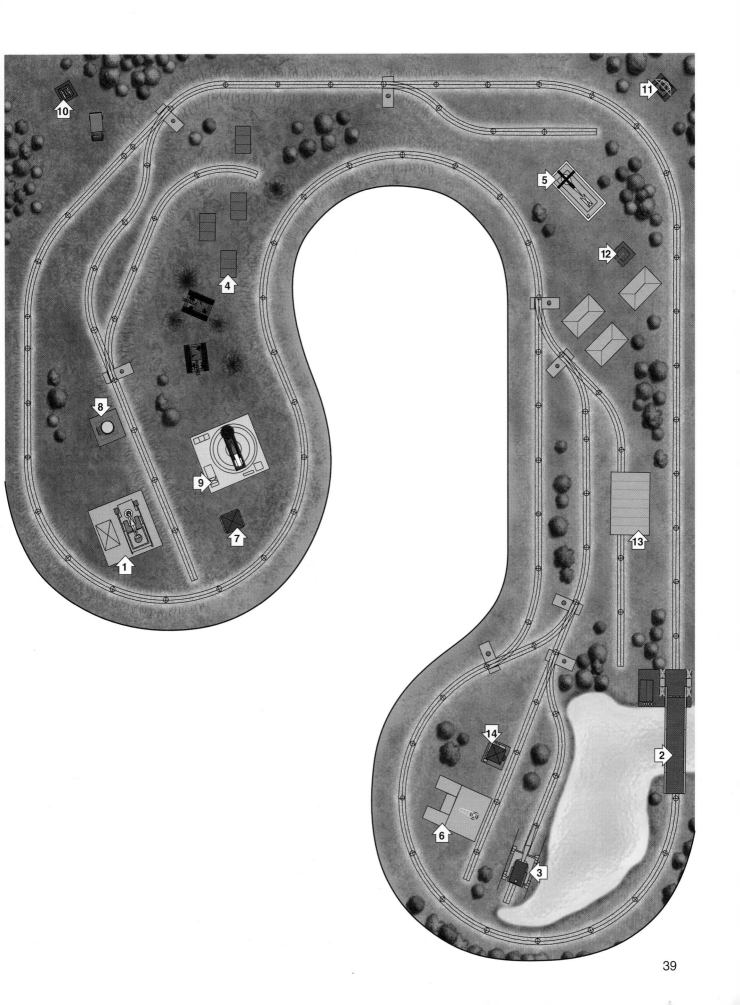

If any of your scale model railroader friends scoff at your searchlight cars and military trains, show them this picture! This is Canadian National car B-1 (B-2 is in the background). The cars were built during World War II to provide defense to coastal routes. Luckily, they never fired a shot in action. Canadian National Railway photo.

several signal towers. On the other side of the layout is a missile-launching facility.

The track list shows the standard Lionel track needed to build this plan. I chose standard track and switches in keeping with the traditional, and fairly whimsical, nature of the accessories. As you can tell from the road name listing, there's no shortage of military rolling stock to operate on this line. In fact, you may even have to dedicate it to just one service. "Okay, Sarge, move 'em out!"

Colorful scenery, a fascinating roster and lots of coal traffic—that sums up the WM. Here, five of the Wild Mary's F units lead a long freight around Helmstetters Curve. Don Phillips photo.

7 Western Maryland
Challengers and Shays on a unique coal-hauling route

For many years the Western Maryland was one of the most popular railroads in the United States among both railfans and modelers. Railfans flocked to the trackside of this medium-sized railroad to photograph its interesting motive power and colorful rolling stock as it wound its way through some of the most beautiful scenery on the North American continent.

The WM was really three railroads in one. A bridge route connected the ocean harbor at Baltimore, Maryland, with the routes that headed inland from Connellsville, Pennsylvania. This was the route of

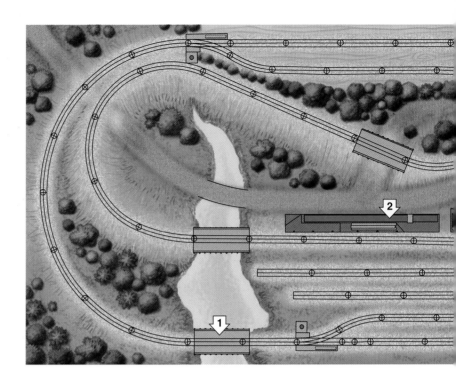

Western Maryland Track

Track
Lionel Single Straight (62)
Lionel Custom-Cut Straight (10)
Lionel O31 Curve 45° (14)
Lionel O54 Curve (17)
Lionel O22 Right-Hand Turnout (4)
Lionel O22 Makeup Straight (5)
Lionel O22 Left-Hand Turnout (6)
Lionel Half Straight (2)
Lionel Cut Stock Curve (5)
Lionel O22 Makeup Curve (3)
K-Line 14-in. Straight (1)

Structures
 1 Lionel 314 Plate Girder Bridge (3)
 2 Lionel 364 Lumber Loader (1)
 3 Lionel 256 Freight Station (1)
 4 Lionel 12904 Coaling Station (1)
 5 Lionel 12733 Watchman's
   Shanty (1)

the famed "Alpha-Jet" freights, so-called because they used a number of smaller eastern railroads to compete with the giants like the Pennsylvania and New York Central. The Western Maryland was also a mountain railroad, with some of the steepest railroad grades in the eastern part of the country. The steep grades and noticeable lack of tangent, or straight, track, helped the railroad earn the nickname "Wild Mary." Finally, the WM was a coal-hauling railroad. From Potomac Junction, Maryland, just outside Cumberland, the line ventured south via the Thomas subdivision into the Appalachian coal fields. In Elkins, West Virginia, the WM connected with the Baltimore & Ohio. Further south, the Thomas sub terminated with the WM's connection with the Chesapeake & Ohio Railroad.

A BRIEF HISTORY

The Western Maryland was incorporated on May 27, 1852, in the city of Baltimore. By the early 1860s, construction had been completed as far west as Gettysburg, Maryland. The Civil War caused a halt in construction, and the line didn't reach Hagerstown until 1872.

Through various leases and acquisitions the WM expanded its holdings in southern Pennsylvania and western Maryland. Wild Mary crossed the Potomac River and entered Cumberland in 1906.

By that time, the city of Baltimore had sold its majority interest in the WM to the Gould syndicate (part of the deal was the extension of the main line to Cumberland and construction of a deep-water port facility, named Port Covington, in Baltimore). The Gould empire collapsed in 1908, driving the WM into receivership. By 1910, the Western Maryland Railway took over and immediately set about extending the line north from Cumberland to a connection with the Pittsburgh & Lake Erie at Connellsville, Pennsylvania.

As early as the 1920s, the Interstate Commerce Commission predicted the future merger of the B&O and the WM. By 1930, the B&O controlled the majority of the WMs stock, although the Western Maryland continued operating as a virtually independent railroad. In the 1950s and '60s the WM reached its peak in terms of traffic and high-speed freight service. As mergers and bankruptcies changed the railroading landscape in the

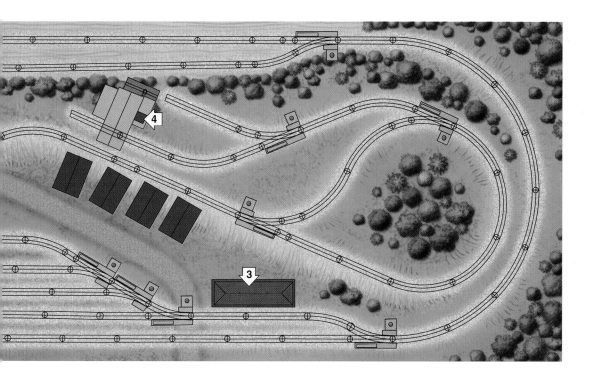

eastern parts of the country, the WM watched its connections disappear. In 1967 the B&O and C&O applied to take over control of the WM. There was little evidence of this control until 1973 with the incorporation of the Chessie System to control the operations of all three railroads.

In late 1983 the B&O merged the Western Maryland. All that remains today are a few of the coal lines along the former Thomas subdivision. But that doesn't mean the Wild Mary can't ride again, at least in a smaller scale.

WILD MARY IN A SPARE ROOM

Western Maryland's twisting route through the Appalachians is ideal for a model railroader who wants to build an interesting layout with some great scenery in a limited space.

Anyone modeling the Western Maryland would want to include at least a hint of the

WM's colorful paint schemes make great toy trains, a fact Lionel has known for years. Here's the 1995 Lionel Service Station set, complete with a low-nose Geep painted in the so-called circus scheme. Darla Evans photo.

Coal was an important part of the Western Maryland's traffic base. To handle the steep grades on some of the coal branches the WM used geared locomotives like Shay no. 6. This engine provided the inspiration for the models from Lionel, Right-of-Way, and Third Rail. P. E. Percy photo.

coal branches, the most notable of which was the Thomas subdivision, as well as depict at least part of the railroad's mainline bridge route. This is really possible, even feasible, within a 5 x 18-foot area.

That 5-foot width is designed to be looked at from one side and both ends. All

you need behind the layout is a narrow access aisle that will make it possible to reach the track and equipment for the infrequent (you hope) maintenance. The mainline loop features O54 curves, which do limit the scenic choices a bit but are the key to operating some of the big-time equipment WM was known for. This was, after all, a railroad that rostered a total of ten 4-6-6-4 Challengers and some big 4-8-4s, called Potomacs on the WM, to keep the fast freights on schedule.

The primary operating feature of the mainline loop is a small interchange yard which connects the main with a coal branch that connects to a couple of coal loaders that keep the hoppers brimming with black diamonds. Upon leaving the main, the branchline crews encounter a twisting and turning right-of-way with O31 curves until they reach the end of the line. A return loop permits the locomotives that operate on the branch, most likely a Lionel low-nose Geep painted in the road's red, white, and black "circus scheme," to head back down the branch front first. Of course if diesels aren't your speed you'll be thrilled to note this layout is the perfect home for Right-of-Way's WM Shay.

A glance at the accompanying table of Western Maryland will confirm the popularity of this little railroad that moved tonnage in a big way. Manifest freights, colorful paint schemes, and coal traffic make the Wild Mary hard to beat.

Western Maryland Trains

Steam Engines
LION	18023	WM Shay "6", 92	
ROW	5009	WM Shay, 92	
ROW	5214	WM 0-4-0 Saddle Tanker, 91	

Diesel Engines
LION	8061	WM/Chessie U36C Powered, orange/blue, 80
LION	18501	WM NW-2 Switcher, 89
LION	18841	WM GP-20 "27" (SSS), 95
MTH	2083	WM F-3 AA Units, 95
MTH	2091	WM F-3 B Unit, 95
MTH	2129	WM BL-2, 96
RED	RC-25	WM GP-9, "speed lettering" scheme, 94
WVR	5506	WM RS-3 "187", 90
WVR	U6570	WM Alco FA-2 Unit "302", 90
WVR	U6571	WM Alco FB-2 Unit "302", 90

Rolling Stock
LION	19214	WM Boxcar (FF #4), 89
LION	9328	WM Chessie Bay Window Caboose, 80
LION	16564	WM Center Cupola Caboose (SSS), 95
LION	19704	WM Wide-vision Caboose, 89
WVR	U2909	WM Northeastern Caboose, 96
LION	17511	WM Flatcars w/ logs, set of 3 (Std O), 95
LION	19404	WM Flatcar w/ trailers,
LION	19403	WM Gondola w/ coal load, 89
LION	16420	WM Quad Hopper w/ coal load (SSS), 95
LION	16424	WM Covered Quad Hopper (SSS), 95
WVR	U2304	WM 3-bay Hopper, 96
LION	16634	WM Coal Dump Car, 91
LION	9818	WM Reefer, black roof/end, 40
LION	19511	WM Reefer, 89
LION	19601	WM 1-D Tank, 89

Position light signals, a unique Pennsylvania Railroad feature, give away the Norfolk & Western's Pennsy heritage. But running Geeps long-hood-forward and long trains of hoppers heading for the sea are uniquely N&W.

8 The Norfolk & Western
Classy coal hauler with a link to the past

If you want to have a classic example of steam power on your railroad, you couldn't choose a better prototype to inspire your modeling than the Norfolk & Western. One look at the N&W's handsome black and maroon 4-8-4 J-class locomotives, or one of the many popular O gauge versions of the same engine, may be all it takes to convert you to a true believer.

But the J's were passenger-hauling engines, and while there's no denying it will make a handsome sight trailing up a string of Tuscan red varnish in its wake, you need to find enough freight traffic to keep the doors open and the trains running. When dealing with the N&W, that's easy. Freight traffic can be summed up in one word: coal.

Although the railroad had lines stretching as far west as St. Louis, the heart of

the N&W has always been the Pocahontas coal fields of West Virginia. The eastern terminal of the N&W, its namesake city of Norfolk, is blessed with one of the finest natural harbors in the world, with access to the Atlantic Ocean. To take advantage of this, the N&W built huge coal-loading piers at Lamberts Point, just about in the middle of downtown Norfolk. In short, a model railroad layout that depicts some of the N&W's interior lies with a small Virginia town, and a representation of the coal piers in Norfolk, would make an interesting and challenging layout to operate. Let's look in more detail at this fascinating railroad.

AN EVOLVING RAILROAD

In an age when American railroads have had to struggle to keep their heads above water, you may be shocked to learn that the Norfolk & Western has actually thrived over the last half century. Prior to 1964, the N&W was a coal-hauling railroad controlled by the mighty Pennsylvania. Much of the N&W's appearance—the position light signals, electrified sections of main line, and Tuscan red passenger equipment—all reflected a Pennsy heritage.

In 1964, perhaps in response to the proposed merger between the Pennsy and the New York Central, the N&W grew up. It acquired the Wabash, Wheeling & Lake Erie, and Akron, Canton & Youngstown. Suddenly, this eastern coal hauler turned into a railroad with a direct route from the eastern seaboard into the heart of the Midwest.

If its Pennsy heritage made the N&W look like a miniature of the Keystone behemoth, N&W's loyalty to its major customer—the coal industry—caused it to keep steam in active daily use much later than every other major U.S. railroad. The railroad built and maintained its steam fleet in its shops in Roanoke, Virginia, and even experimented with a coal-burning steam turbine-electric locomotive aptly christened *Jawn Henry*.

In the first half of the twentieth century most of the N&W's coal traffic was westbound, toward the Great Lakes. But in the mid-1950s demand grew in Europe for high-grade coal. This meant N&W coal trains had to face several steep climbs on their way to the port of Norfolk. But the Virginian Railway, which ran parallel to the N&W, had a much gentler grade. The

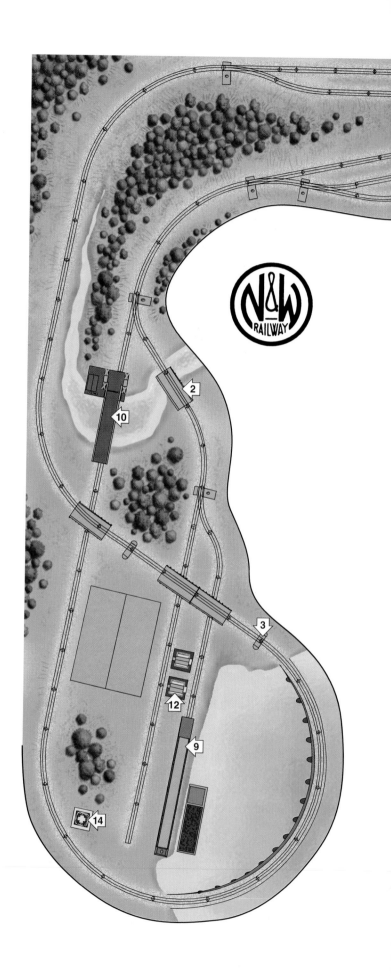

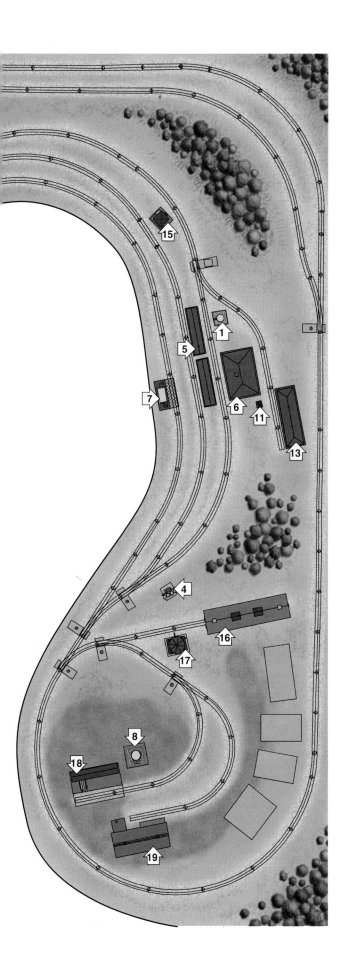

Norfolk & Western Pier 6 juts 1,600 feet into Norfolk harbor. Here coal is loaded into colliers for transport overseas. Norfolk & Western photo.

Norfolk & Western Track
Track
Lionel O72 Curve 22.5° (55)
Lionel Single Straight (85)
Lionel Cut Stock Curve (7)
Lionel O72 Left-Hand Turnout (3)
Lionel Custom-Cut Straight (8)
Lionel O72 Right-Hand Turnout (3)
Lionel O31 Modern Right-Hand Turnout (3)
Lionel O31 Curve 45° (7)
Lionel Half Straight (5)
Lionel O31 Modern Left-Hand Turnout (2)
Lionel O31 Prewar O11 Left-Hand Turnout (1)
Lionel O54 Curve (2)
K-Line 14-in. Straight (1)

Structures
1 Lionel 93 Water Tower (1)
2 Lionel 314 Plate Girder Bridge (4)
3 Lionel Bridge Trestle (2)
4 Lionel 195 Floodlight Tower (1)
5 Lionel 156 Freight Platform (2)
6 Lionel 133 Passenger Station (1)
7 Lionel 3462P Milk Car Platform (1)
8 Lionel 193 Industrial Water Tower (1)
9 Lionel 456 Coal Ramp (1)
10 Lionel 313 Bascule Bridge (1)
11 Lionel 75 Goose-neck Lamp (1)
12 Lionel 98 Coal Bunker (2)
13 Lionel 356 Operating Freight Station (1)
14 Lionel 395 Floodlight Tower (yellow) (1)
15 Lionel 12733 Watchman's Shanty (1)
16 Lionel 12897 Engine House (1)
17 Lionel 12711 Water Tower (1)
18 Lionel 12798 Forklift Loader (1)
19 Lionel 12905 Factory (1)

It's September 1957 and the westbound *Powahatan Arrow* rockets past behind J-class 4-8-4 no. 604. When you get sick of the coal traffic, just sit back and let your J roar past. John Krave photo.

Norfolk & Western Trains

Steam Engines

LION	746	Streamlined 4-8-4 Steam, die-cast body, 57–60
LION	18040	N&W 4-8-4 "612", orange/yellow stripe, 95
MTH	1105	N&W 4-8-4 J Northern (O27), 96
MTH	1111	N&W USRA 0-8-0 (O27), 96
3RD	No Number	N&W 4-8-2, streamlined, 97
WMS	5601	N&W 4-8-4 J, 90
WMS	BS07	N&W Class A 2-6-6-4, 96

Diesel Engines

LION	8266	N&W SD-24 Powered w/horn, 82
LION	8763	N&W GP-9 Powered, 76–78
MTH	2014	N&W Alco C30-7, 94
RED	RC-05	N&W GP-9, 94
WVR	5505	N&W RS-3 "301", 90
WMS	2311	N&W FM Trainmaster Units, 81–96

Rolling Stock

LION	9129	N&W Auto Carrier, white lettering, 75–76
LION	9205	N&W Boxcar, white letters, 70
LION	9604	N&W Hi-cube, silver door, 76–77
MTH	9103	N&W Caboose (Std O), 96
3RD	OG3RCAB	N&W USRA Caboose, 96
WVR	U2907	N&W Northeastern Caboose, 96
LION	16360	N&W Maxi-Stack Flatcar set w/ containers, 93
MTH	7206	N&W Gondola w/ crates, 96
LION	6446-25	N&W Quad Hopper, 70
LION	17109	N&W ACF 3-bay Hopper, black letters (Std O), 91
MTH	7506	N&W Hopper, black, 96
WVR	U1109	N&W 2-bay Hopper, 90

Passenger Cars

LION	19142	N&W Passenger Car "538", 95
LION	19151	N&W Duplex Roomette Car, 96
MTH	6014	N&W 60' Streamlined Passenger Car, set of 4, 96
WMS	M223	N&W Madison Passenger set, red, 82–95

N&W had applied to the Interstate Commerce Commission to lease the VGN in 1925, but the application was denied. But in 1959, when the N&W tried again, the merger was approved with nary a whisper of protest. Although the VGN had operated a fairly extensive length of electrified service, a one-way traffic pattern made the electrified service a thing of the past and the wires came down in 1962. The Virginian's newest electrics, the EF-4s, were sold to the New Haven to restore electrified freight service on that railroad.

By 1990 the Norfolk & Western merged with the Southern Railway to form Norfolk Southern. Even in today's world of mega-mergers, the NS remains a fiercely independent, and highly successful, railroad.

THE N&W IN A GARAGE

The track plan includes many of the elements that made the Norfolk & Western a unique railroad, combined with a continuous-run main line that features fairly gentle grades and O72 curves. The plan as shown will require an area of 16 x 18 feet—about half of a two-car garage or the basement of a small Cape Cod–style house.

One of the two main line lobes features a typical Virginia town, with a classy brick station and long platforms that will make a great setting for your J-class Northern steam locomotive and a string of matching Tuscan red passenger cars. A small engine facility, a factory combined with a culvert loader, and a milk-car-operating platform complete this image of Virginia small-town living.

The second lobe can feature a large coal breaker and loader like that shown in the prototype photo included with the Western Maryland track plan. Or you can do as we have done and incorporate the Lionel coal ramp into your own version of Lamberts Point.

Heavy traffic, classy passenger trains pulled by a classic Lionel postwar beauty, and interesting accessories make the Norfolk & Western a real winner for a prototype-based toy train layout.

The Standard Railroad of the World may be the perfect choice for a prototype for your next toy train layout. You can recreate the action of the Pennsy, such as this pair of Baldwin Sharks as they depart Terre Haute, Indiana, on the point of the *American.* Wayne P. Ellis photo.

9 The Pennsylvania RR
Tuscan giant

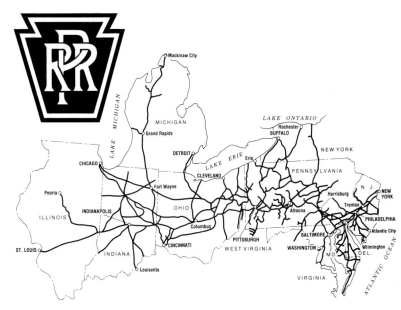

Few other American companies have risen to the prominence once attained by the Pennsylvania Railroad. In its glory days, the PRR was the richest corporation in the world. This line was, by its own proclamation, the Standard Railroad of the World. And while the Pennsy did bring standardization to everything it touched, it didn't see eye to eye with virtually every other railroad on the continent. The result was equipment, signals, and even right-of-way that had a distinctive Pennsy look to it.

Perhaps the line's greatest era was during World War II. At that time passenger trains were hauled behind a fleet of 425

49

K-4s class 4-6-2s. Freight was hauled behind 5790 L1 class Mikados.

Everything on Pennsy was designed, approved, tested, and in many cases built by the railroad's engineering and shop forces. Much of this standardization was different from every other railroad in North America: Belpaire fireboxes on steamers, position light signals, boxcars taller than everyone else's.

The Pennsylvania Railroad seemed invincible, but truth is sometimes stranger than fiction. In 1957 Pennsy and arch-rival New York Central announced plans to merge. The two railroads ran parallel routes and served many of the same cities. The merger was finalized on February 1, 1968. The new railroad, called Penn Central, was an object lesson in how not to run a railroad. PC absorbed the New Haven into its quagmire before it sank into the greatest bankruptcy in U.S. history to that point. Penn Central would eventually rise from the ashes as part of Conrail, but the mighty PRR was no more.

THE STANDARD RAILROAD OF THE WORLD

Although much of the Pennsy's equipment was unique, the railroad has always enjoyed a large following. This means many specific Pennsy models have been made available, and many toy trains are based on Pennsy prototypes. There are reasonably well crafted toy train models of Pennsy's N5c cabin car, the K4 steam locomotive, and even the Pennsy's S2 turbine. In recent years, many manufacturers such as Weaver, Williams, and Third Rail have offered detailed models of Pennsy steam power. The table shows a listing of the other models that have been made for Pennsy over the years.

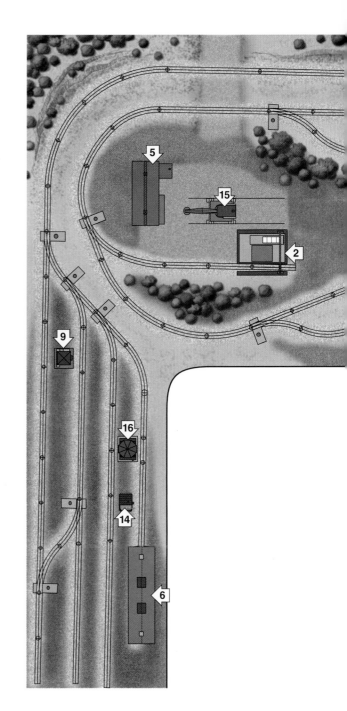

PRR M-1 no. 6901 races through East Rochester, Ohio, in this view. In the distance is a coaling dock spanning the tracks. These were quite common on Pennsy Midwest lines and one has been included on the track plan. G. G. Grabill, Jr.

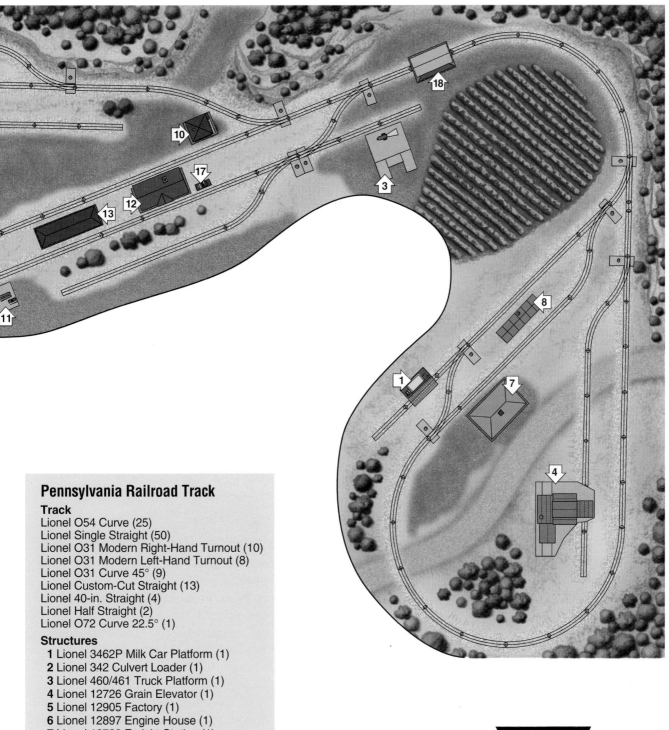

Pennsylvania Railroad Track

Track
Lionel O54 Curve (25)
Lionel Single Straight (50)
Lionel O31 Modern Right-Hand Turnout (10)
Lionel O31 Modern Left-Hand Turnout (8)
Lionel O31 Curve 45° (9)
Lionel Custom-Cut Straight (13)
Lionel 40-in. Straight (4)
Lionel Half Straight (2)
Lionel O72 Curve 22.5° (1)

Structures
 1 Lionel 3462P Milk Car Platform (1)
 2 Lionel 342 Culvert Loader (1)
 3 Lionel 460/461 Truck Platform (1)
 4 Lionel 12726 Grain Elevator (1)
 5 Lionel 12905 Factory (1)
 6 Lionel 12897 Engine House (1)
 7 Lionel 12728 Freight Station (1)
 8 Lionel 12773 Freight Platform (1)
 9 Lionel 12733 Watchman's Shanty (1)
10 Lionel 12768 Burning Switch Tower (1)
11 Lionel 12892 Automatic Gateman (1)
12 Lionel 12734 Passenger/Freight Station (1)
13 Lionel 2129 Freight Station (1)
14 Lionel 12718 Barrel Shed (1)
15 Lionel 12834 PRR Gantry Crane (1)
16 Lionel 12711 Water Tower (1)
17 Lionel 12729 Mail Pickup (1)
18 Lionel 2315 Coaling Station (1)

East of Pittsburgh the Pennsy was a heavy-duty multitrack railroad, but in Indiana and Ohio the pace was less hectic. A set of E7s leads the *Buckeye* through Logansport, Indiana. Louis A. Marre photo.

Pennsylvania Railroad Trains

Steam Engines
LION	8404	PRR 6-8-6 Steam, gray trim, 84–85
MTH	1115	PRR K4s 4-6-2 Pacific (O27), 97
ROW	5204	PRR 0-4-0 Saddle Tanker, 91
3RD	OG3R3	PRR S2 6-8-6 Turbine, 94
WVR	1071	PRR L1 2-8-2 Mikado, 93
WMS	5200	PRR B6 0-6-0 Switcher, 87

Diesel Engines
LION	18307	PRR Train Master, gold lettering, "8699", 94
LION	18832	PRR RSD-4, 6-wheel, yellow lettering, "8446", 95
MTH	2071	PRR GP-30, 95
MTH	2133	PRR AS-616, 96
RED	RC-07	PRR GP-9, Brunswick green, 94
WVR	1404	PRR RF-16 Sharknose AB Units, Tuscan red w/ 5 stripes, 94
WMS	46	PRR Might Mite Switcher, green, 84

Electric Engines
LION	8272	PRR EP-5, gold ends/striping, 82
MTH	2121	PRR GG-1, Tuscan red (O27), 96
3RD	3RP5A	PRR P-5a Electric, 97

Motorized Units
LION	18306	PRR MU Car set, Powered and Dummy "4574", 92
WMS	RDC213	PRR Budd RDC, set of 3, 96

Rolling Stock
MTH	7408	PRR Merchandise Boxcar, Tuscan red, 96
3RD	OG3RBOX	PRR WWII Emergency Boxcar, 96
3RD	OG3RCAB	PRR USRA Caboose, 96
WVR	U2901	PRR Northeastern Caboose, 96
WMS	FC06	PRR Stock Car, Tuscan red, 93–95
MTH	7200	PRR Gondola, 95
WVR	U1106	PRR 2-bay Hopper, black, 90
LION	19320	PRR Ore w/ load, 92
MTH	7800	PRR Reefer, 95
MTH	7300	PRR Tank Car, 95

Passenger Cars
ROW	3504	PRR Passenger Car, set of 6, 92
WVR	1123	PRR Passenger Cars, set of 2, 93
WMS	M105	PRR Madison Passenger set, Tuscan red, 75–92

The track plan is a fairly simple continuous-run schematic that includes two small towns, complete with trackside industries you'd expect to find in small towns in places like Indiana and Ohio. We'll take advantage of the space available along the wall to provide a small yard. The yard lead wraps around and behind the main line so, with luck, the yard crew won't interfere with the road engines as they roar by on their way to Chicago or Pittsburgh.

There are a number of places where you can enjoy watching a variety of accessories in action, but most of this layout is fairly spread out. After the benchwork is up and the track is operating smoothly, you can start adding all the little details that will make this look like the Pennsy to all knowledgeable viewers. Flip through the pages of the Kalmbach book *Heart of the Pennsylvania Railroad, The Main Line: Philadelphia to Pittsburgh,* by Robert S. McGonigal, and you'll quickly see evidence of the standardization that is not only fun to add but gives your railroad a flavor all its own.

Small towns, classic Tuscan red passenger cars, and elegantly pinstriped diesels will let you re-create the glory that was the Standard Railroad of the World in your basement.

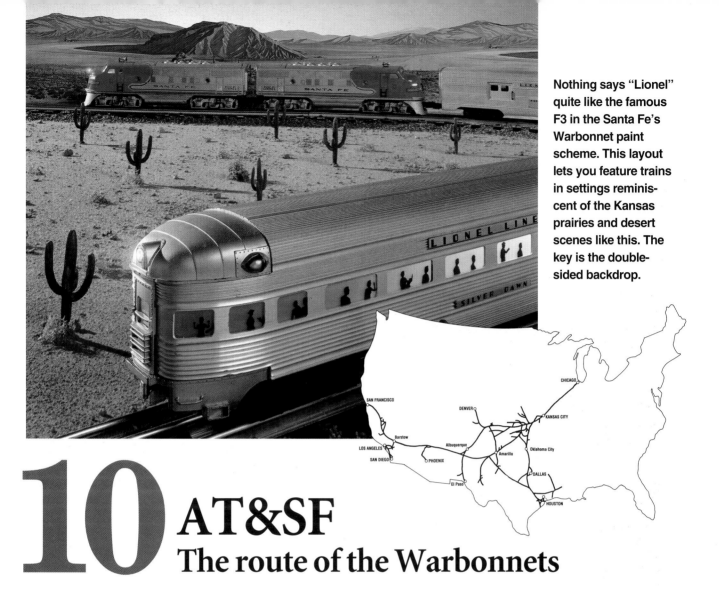

Nothing says "Lionel" quite like the famous F3 in the Santa Fe's Warbonnet paint scheme. This layout lets you feature trains in settings reminiscent of the Kansas prairies and desert scenes like this. The key is the double-sided backdrop.

10 AT&SF
The route of the Warbonnets

The Atchison, Topeka & Santa Fe passed through lots of hometowns and backyards on its route from Chicago to Los Angeles, so it should come as no surprise that it's always been a popular prototype railroad among modelers. But it could be argued that the Lionel Corp. had boosted the popularity of this line when it released its red and silver warbonnet F3—quite possibly the most recognizable toy train of all time and the image that leaps to the mind of most people when they hear the name "Lionel."

Since the initial release of the F3 in the postwar years, Lionel has also released updated versions of the same paint scheme (command-control ready with RailSoundsII) and even brought out a freight version of the F3, complete with the more subtle, but no less attractive, blue and yellow colors.

But can a toy train operator who wants to capture the magic of Santa Fe country, complete with desert scenes, Spanish mission–style station buildings, and handsome F3s pulling glittering trains of streamliners, manage to fit everything into a relatively humble area? Take a look at the track plan here, and let's see what's possible.

WIDE OPEN SPACES

The Santa Fe recently merged with the Burlington Northern to form Burlington Northern Santa Fe, but a railroad that's as ingrained into the heart of the industry as this one seems destined to live on. The road dates back to 1859. Its original purpose, to link two of its namesake cities in Kansas with Santa Fe, New Mexico, seems foolhardy today, but through acquisition and further expansion the line eventually

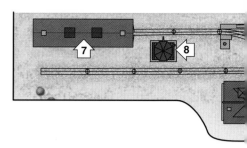

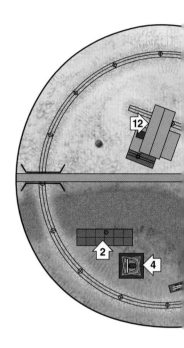

AT&SF Track

Track	Structures
Lionel O54 Curve (41)	1 Lionel 12709 Banjo Signal (2)
Lionel Single Straight (40)	2 Lionel 12773 Freight Platform (1)
Lionel Custom-Cut Straight (7)	3 Lionel 62709 Rico Station (1)
Lionel O72 Curve 22.5° (11)	4 Lionel 12889 Motorized Windmill (1)
Lionel O22 Right-Hand Turnout (6)	5 Lionel/MPC 2783 Freight Station (1)
Lionel O22 Makeup Straight (5)	6 Lionel 12729 Mail Pickup (1)
Lionel O42 Curve 30° (8)	7 Lionel 12897 Engine House (1)
Lionel Cut Stock Curve (3)	8 Lionel 12711 Water Tower (1)
Lionel O22 Left-Hand Turnout (3)	9 Lionel 12917 Operating Switch Tower (1)
Lionel 40-in. Straight (3)	10 Lionel 2115 Dwarf Block Signal (2)
Lionel Half Straight (3)	11 Lionel 2163 Block Signal (1)
Lionel O72 Left-Hand Turnout (1)	12 Lionel 12904 Coaling Station (1)

passed through Albuquerque, New Mexico (Santa Fe was relegated to the end of short branch), and reached the Pacific coast. Expansion east and north to Chicago and the numerous connections in that area turned the AT&SF into a major transcontinental link.

Santa Fe was well known to shippers and travelers, but it really wasn't until after the Second World War that the line gained widespread attention from the railfan community. Since long stretches of the Santa Fe main line traverse areas without water, the Santa Fe was one of the first major railroads to dieselize both its passenger and freight service. The silver and red paint scheme chosen for the passenger engines was complemented by matching stainless-steel passenger equipment. Trains like the *Chief* and *Super Chief* gained renown with the traveling public and were considered the way to travel to the west coast in the postwar years.

But the speed of airline travel and the introduction of the interstate highway system had the same effect on the Santa Fe as on other railroads, and by the mid-60s the passenger trade had all but vanished.

Blue and yellow freight engines, some wearing a modified version of the warbonnet, dominated the Santa Fe roster for years. With the onset of intermodal traffic, which Santa Fe quickly made a significant part of its traffic, speed and reliability were once again an important part of the railroad's operation.

To reflect the importance of intermodal travel, Santa Fe ordered its newest high-horsepower freight locomotives painted in a modified version of the classic red and silver warbonnet. Although today more

Here is a Super C high-speed piggyback train on its inaugural run (note the passenger cars in the consist for official guests) through Gallup, New Mexico, on January 18, 1968. Santa Fe Railway Public Relations Department photo.

and more engines are being painted the green and orange of the BNSF, it's hard to imagine the world without the classic red and silver.

WE'RE NOT IN KANSAS ANYMORE. . . . OR ARE WE?

Compressing the mighty 12,000 mile Santa Fe into a 13 x 19-foot room may seem virtually impossible. We won't try to capture the entire system, but instead we'll use a technique that's proven remarkably effective on many scale layouts to show both the Santa Fe's Kansas origins and the wide-open mesas of the southwest as a setting for this layout.

Schematically, our plan is a continuous-run oval with a small stub-ended yard along one wall. The oval has been twisted up and over itself to both lengthen the run and provide a more interesting route for the main line. This routing doesn't come free—to fit it the area provided for

the layout we need to tighten some of the curves. This is no real problem if you want to run F3s and shortened Lionel passenger cars, but if your tastes run to scale-length 80-foot passenger car sets and modern six-axle diesels, you may want to adopt another plan that offers O72 minimums.

Desert isn't the only scenery found along the Santa Fe. Kansas also plays host to the AT&SF, as you can see in this shot taken in Matfield Green, Kansas, in July 1983. Joe McMillan photo.

Equipment

Steam Engines

LION	8900	AT&SF 4-6-4 Steam, silver front, 79
MTH	3013	AT&SF 4-8-4 Northern "2903", 95
3RD	OG3RSF	Santa Fe 2-8-0 Consolidation, 96
WVR	1076	Santa Fe 4-6-4 "Blue Goose" Hudson, 94
WMS	5007	AT&SF USRA 4-6-2 Pacific, 89

Diesel Engines

LION	18801	Santa Fe U36B "8801", 87
MTH	2077	AT&SF H10-44, 95
RED	RC-59	Santa Fe GP-9, "zebra" stripe, 94
3RD	No Number	Santa Fe Dash C44-9W, silver/red,
WVR	1304	Santa Fe/SP SD-40-2 "5068", 93
WMS	FM220	Santa Fe FM Trainmaster Units, silver/red,

Motorized Units

LION	18405	Santa Fe Burro Crane, 89
WMS	BC203	Santa Fe Budd RDC, set of 3, 95

Rolling Stock

LION	16253	Santa Fe Auto Carrier, yellow stripe, 94
LION	6464-700	Santa Fe Boxcar, white lettering, 61–66
LION	5717	AT&SF Bunk Car, 83
MTH	9105	Santa Fe Caboose (Std O), 97
MTH	7108	Santa Fe Stock Car, 96
MTH	7603	Santa Fe Flatcar, 95
ROW	385526	Santa Fe Well Car w/ containers,
WVR	U2608	Santa Fe 50' Bulkhead Flatcar, 95
LION	6258	AT&SF Gondola, two silver canisters, 85–92
MTH	7503	Santa Fe Hopper, 95–96
3RD	OG3RHOP	Santa Fe 50-ton 2-bay Hopper, 96
WVR	U1605	Santa Fe 4-bay ACF Hopper, 90–95
LION	17302	Santa Fe Reefer, w/ end-of-train device (Std O), 90
LION	17900	Santa Fe Tank Car, black, white letters (Std O),

Passenger Cars

MTH	4017	Santa Fe 80' Madison Cars, set of 5, 96
ROW	3500	Santa Fe Passenger Car, set of 6, 91
WVR	1121	Santa Fe Passenger Cars, set of 2, 93
WMS	M231	Santa Fe Madison Passenger set, silver/red, 95

The stub-ended yard provides an interesting place to classify cars before they head out onto the main line, and the double-ended siding will let you pull the road engines off the head end of arriving trains so you won't have power getting stranded. There's no room for it here, but if you have more space for the layout you may want to consider lengthening the yard lead—that way the yard operator won't be constantly fouling the main line.

Most of the switches are new Lionel 23010 and 23011 components, which allow a closer spacing between parallel tracks than the old O31 variety. The key to creating the wide-open country look is the double-sided backdrop that runs down the center of the peninsula. You don't have to be an artist to make a backdrop. In fact, the less detail on the backdrop the better. After all, you want people to look at the trains, not pay attention to the backdrop. A simple coat of sky blue latex paint will do. If you want to find out more about backdrops, I would certainly recommend the Kalmbach publication *Realistic Scenery for Toy Train Layouts,* by Dave Frary.

But even a simple backdrop can add a lot of variety to the layout. Since the backdrop keeps the scenes visually distinct, one side of the peninsula can have a Kansas farm town with a grain elevator and horse loader, and the other side can feature the much more arid scenery typical of the southwest. On the Kansas side of the layout we've included a small wooden station, and a mission-style station will add lots of interest to the southwestern scene. This station can be a stock plastic kit, or you can scratchbuild a Santa Fe mission-style station, complete with a red tile roof.

The table shows a taste of the equipment made for the Santa Fe over the years. There's almost an embarrassment of riches, so whether your interests lean towards the glory days of the '50s streamliners, or the modern-day stack trains with their modern high-horsepower diesels, you'll find lots of interesting projects along the route of the Warbonnet.

The unmistakable outline of the Empire State Building removes all doubt as to the locale. The elevated line helps save space on a layout, since you can put city scenery below the tracks. New York Central RS-3 no. 8350 has just dropped 35 cars of mail at the post office. Jim Shaughnessy photo.

11

The New York Central's West Side Line
Gotham in a garage

Traditional toy train layouts usually feature lots of track, accessories, and other elements crammed into a limited area. Let's face it—most toy train layouts don't look anything like the prairies of Kansas or the wild Appalachians. Perhaps the secret to finding a theme for a toy train layout is to look not at the open country but at the congested city. Let's throw caution to the winds and choose one of the biggest: New York.

When railfans and modelers think of the New York Central, the mighty Water Level Route north of New York City along the banks of the Hudson River leaps to mind. This was the stomping ground of mighty Niagaras and Dreyfuss Hudsons and the path that the famed *20th Century Limited* followed into the Big Apple. But the NYC was more than just a Hudson River Valley speedway. Perhaps some of the most fascinating lines of this massive far-flung empire were found on the west side of Manhattan island.

NYC'S WEST SIDE LINE
The Wide Side line was a freight-only line that darted through, under, and

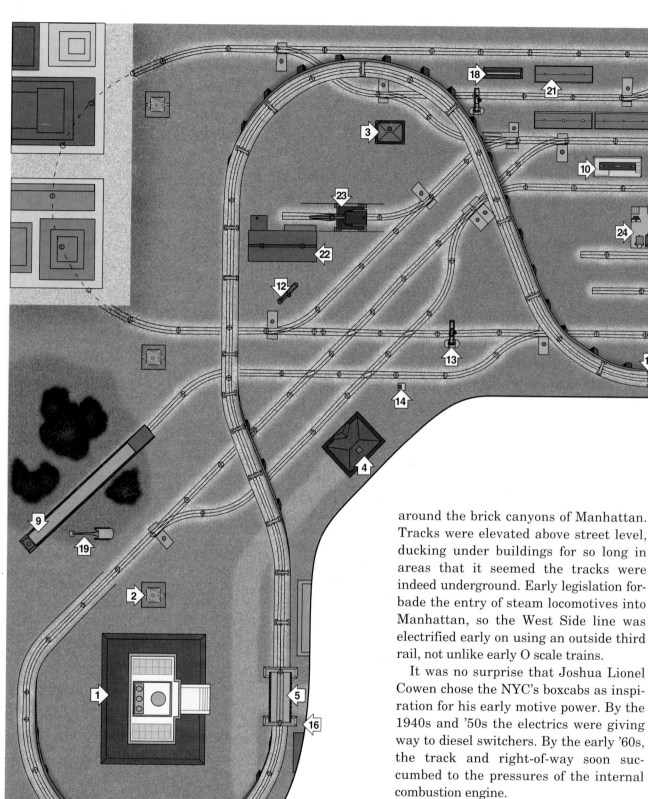

around the brick canyons of Manhattan. Tracks were elevated above street level, ducking under buildings for so long in areas that it seemed the tracks were indeed underground. Early legislation forbade the entry of steam locomotives into Manhattan, so the West Side line was electrified early on using an outside third rail, not unlike early O scale trains.

It was no surprise that Joshua Lionel Cowen chose the NYC's boxcabs as inspiration for his early motive power. By the 1940s and '50s the electrics were giving way to diesel switchers. By the early '60s, the track and right-of-way soon succumbed to the pressures of the internal combustion engine.

Today, a few vestiges of the once extensive sets of lines remain on the West Side, and the island of Manhattan suffers from a condition best described as terminal highway gridlock.

Even more interesting than the line itself is how the NYC transported cars into

The New York Central's West Side freight line provided service to a number of industrial customers throughout Manhattan. To avoid the city streets, most of the right-of-way was elevated above the streets—meaning that many of the industries had their railroad freight doors on the second or third floor! New York Central photo.

New York Central Track

Track
Lionel O54 Curve (35)
Lionel Single Straight (76)
Lionel 45° Cross (4)
Lionel O31 Curve 45° (12)
Lionel O31 Modern Right-Hand Turnout (10)
Lionel O31 Modern Left-Hand Turnout (9)
Lionel Half Straight (4)
Lionel Custom-Cut Straight (12)
Lionel Cut Stock Curve (1)
Lionel O72 Curve 22.5° (1)
Lionel O22 Left-Hand Turnout (1)
Lionel O22 Makeup Curve (1)

Structures
1 Lionel 840 Power Station (1)
2 Lionel 94 High-tension Tower (3)
3 Lionel 438 Signal Tower (1)
4 Lionel 437 Switch Tower (1)

5 Lionel 214 Plate Girder Bridge (1)
6 Lionel 128 Newsstand (1)
7 Lionel 115 Lionel City Station (1)
8 Lionel 352 Ice Depot (1)
9 Lionel 456 Coal Ramp (1)
10 Lionel 334 Operating Dispatching Board (1)
11 Lionel 114 Newsstand with Horn (1)
12 Lionel 310 Billboard w/ 410 Blinker Light (1)
13 Lionel 452 Gantry Signal (2)
14 Lionel 148 Dwarf Block Signal (1)
15 Lionel 12754 Trestle (17)
16 Lionel 12744 Rock Pier (2)
17 Lionel 12898 Flagpole (1)
18 Lionel 12761 Animated Billboard (1)
19 Lionel 12901 Steam Shovel (1)
20 Lionel 12722 Roadside Diner (1)
21 Lionel 12748 Illuminated Station Platform (6)
22 Lionel 12905 Factory (1)
23 Lionel 12922 NYC Gantry Crane (1)
24 Lionel 12862 Oil Drum Loader (1)

and out of Manhattan. While passenger trains had ready access to downtown via Grand Central Terminal, the lowly freight car normally arrived in New York City riding one of a massive fleet of railroad barges and tugs.

GOTHAM IN A GARAGE

This 14 x 18-foot L-shaped plan will fit comfortably in a 1½ car garage or a medium-sized basement. You'll need to access the layout from all sides. Although there are some O31 curves present on the

NYC shared the Grand Central Terminal with the New Haven, which also headed cross town via a different route to connect with the Pennsylvania Railroad at Penn Station. Jim Shaughnessy photo.

New York Central Trains

Steam Engines
LION	773	Steam 4-6-4 Hudson w/ 773W Tender, 64–66
MTH	1113	NYC 4-6-4 Dreyfuss Hudson (O27), 96
3RD	No Number	NYC 2-8-0 Consolidation, 97
WVR	1024	NYC 0-6-0 Switcher, 92
WMS	5602	NYC 4-8-4 Niagara, 90

Diesel Engines
LION	2344	NYC F-3 AA Units, two-tone, white trim, 50–52
MTH	2018	NYC Alco PA-1 AA Units, two-tone gray,
RED	RC-03	NYC GP-9, lightning stripe, 94
WVR	1402	NYC RF-16 Sharknose AB Units, 94
WMS	4620	NYC FM Trainmaster Units, two-tone gray, 83–96

Electric Engines
3RD	No Number	NYC 4-6-6-4 Electric, 96

Motorized Units
LION	18436	NYC Dodge Ram Track Inspection Vehicle, 97
WMS	BC201	NYC Budd RDC, set of 3, 95

Rolling Stock
LION	6464-510	NYC Pacemaker Boxcar, yellow door, 57–58
MTH	7401	NYC Boxcar, 95
WVR	U2106	NYC 40' Boxcar, 95
LION	16703	NYC Tool Car, gray, black letters,
WMS	730	NYC Caboose, Tuscan red (Std O), 93
MTH	7904	NYC Stock w/ cow sounds, N/A
WMS	FC10	NYC Stock Car, green, 93–95
LION	6579	NYC Crane, white lettering, 85–86
WVR	U2506	NYC 50' Flatcar, 95
LION	9824	NYC Gondola, (Std. O), 75–76
MTH	7201	NYC Gondola, 95
MTH	7501	NYC Hopper, 95
LION	9815	NYC Reefer (Std. O), Tuscan roof, 84–85
MTH	7301	NYC Tank Car, 95

Passenger Cars
WVR	1226	NYC Passenger Cars, two-tone gray, set of 5 (Std O), 93
WMS	M102	NYC Madison Passenger set, two-tone gray, 82–94

layout, it's easy enough to set up one route with a minimum radius of O54. The passenger station is elevated above the track level. This not only helps capture the look of the city, it gives you a chance to have at least one corner of the layout uncluttered with track. Clutter that area with buildings, streets, and mini-scenes instead.

A diner and a newsstand, complete with its dog and fire hydrant, are located across the street from the station building. A number of operating accessories are located throughout the layout, including an extensive array of passenger platforms that may look like overkill until you consider how long the platform tracks in Penn Station and Grand Central really are!

The New York Central was Lionel's hometown railroad, in spirit at least. For many years some real classics joined the Hudson and boxcabs. Most notable was the lightning stripe F3. Today, contemporary manufacturers such as MTH, Weaver, and Williams produce Alcos, Sharknoses, Pacemaker boxcars, and much more to complete a list of equipment that seems to revive that of the real road.

A wide variety of equipment, exciting accessories, and the greatest town on earth. And just think, all the thrill of New York—without the crowds and traffic. Even King Kong didn't have it so good.

Wide spaces between tracks make intermodal terminals easy to identify. Lionel's intermodal crane makes it easy for toy train operators to capture the excitement of this modern form of transportation. This is the Sea-Land terminal in Tacoma, Washington. Sea-Land photo.

12 Intermodal Terminal

Spend a few minutes trackside, and you'll notice that today's freight trains don't look much like the trains of years ago. For one thing, the locomotives are much bigger and more powerful than ever before. Trains may not be as numerous as they once were, but they tend to be longer and run at higher average speeds than at any other point in the history of railroading.

The major cause of this change has been the increased popularity of intermodal traffic. Intermodal is a simple concept that has radically changed transportation. The

Intermodal Terminal Track

Track
Lionel O72 Curve 22.5° (24)
Lionel O72 Right-Hand Turnout (5)
Lionel Single Straight (55)
Lionel O72 Left-Hand Turnout (3)
Lionel O31 Modern Right-Hand Turnout (7)
Lionel 40-in. Straight (7)
Lionel Custom-Cut Straight (15)
Lionel O31 Curve 45° (2)
Lionel O31 Modern Left-Hand Turnout (3)

Structures
 1 Lionel 193 Industrial Water Tower (1)
 2 Lionel 12798 Forklift Loader (1)
 3 Lionel 12741 UP Intermodal Crane (2)
 4 Lionel 12905 Factory (1)
 5 Lionel 2710 Billboard (3)
 6 Lionel 2324 Operating Switch Tower (1)
 7 Lionel 12782 Operating Lift Bridge (1)
 8 Lionel 12878 Illuminated Control Tower (1)
 9 Lionel 12733 Watchman's Shanty (1)
 10 Lionel 12884 Truck Loading Dock (1)
 11 Lionel 12734 Passenger/Freight Station (1)
 12 Lionel 12748 Illuminated Station Platform (5)
 13 Lionel 12927 Yard Light (1)
 14 Lionel 12759 Floodlight (1)
 15 Lionel 2195 Floodlight Tower (1)
 16 Lionel 2314 Searchlight (1)
 17 Lionel 2115 Dwarf Block Signal (1)
 18 Lionel 12763 Single Gantry Signal (1)
 19 Lionel 2302 UP Gantry Crane (2)

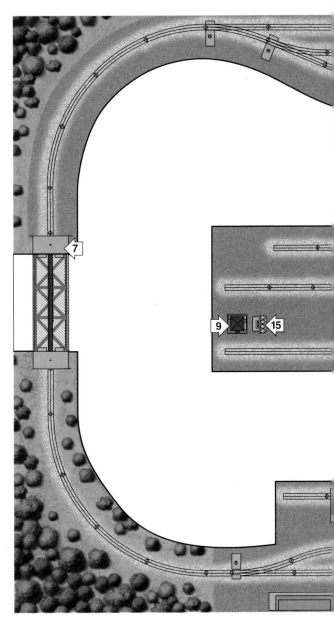

At the Southern Pacific's container terminal in Los Angeles, big overhead gantry cranes lift containers from trucks and onto specially designed rail cars called well cars. Rapid loading and unloading of entire trains makes it viable for railroads to compete with trucks. Southern Pacific Co. photo.

leading advantage of containerization is the fact that a shipper can load goods into a container, seal the container, and then transport it anywhere in the world without having to unload the container until it reaches its final destination.

Containers are built to standard sizes, and they can be loaded onto trailers to be pulled by trucks, onto railroad flatcars or special container train cars called well cars, and even onto ships. This one development has pumped a great deal of new life and energy into railroading, and railroads maintain large container terminals

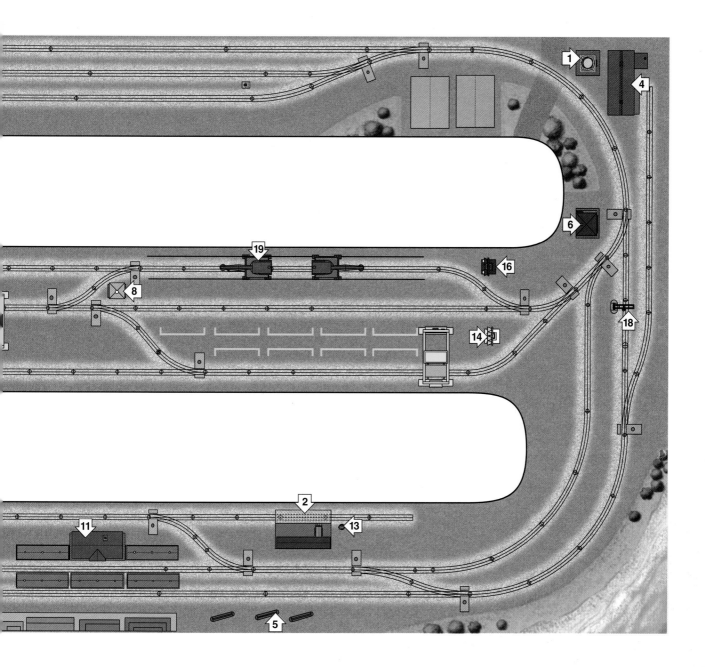

at virtually every major city and harbor. Here trains are loaded with containers and dispatched literally minutes apart at peak hours to race their way across the country.

Lionel makes it easy to depict a container terminal on a toy train layout with their intermodal crane. This accessory lets you pick containers up and set them down and actually load them onto the train.

CROSSROADS OF COMMERCE

Modern intermodal facilities bear little resemblance to the classification yards of even 20 years ago. At first glance, an

intermodal yard looks as if somebody goofed and put all the tracks too far apart. But that's no goof—it's quite intentional, and to understand why, it's helpful to know how a yard functions.

While each installation is unique, the function of every yard is the same: to load and unload containers onto and off trains as fast and safely as possible. Most container traffic arrives via ship or truck. Even at many ports, the containers are moved to the railhead by means of small tractors. The tractors park the containers parallel to the loading tracks (the reason

A single Conrail SD60M leads a string of 67 RoadRailers into Danville, Virginia. New O gauge Road-Railer models from Bowser and a Conrail SD60M from Lionel or MTH make it easy to replicate modern intermodal trains. Curt Tillotson photo.

for the extra room between tracks), one behind the other. The intermodal cranes then move their way down the line, picking up the containers and lifting them into position on the train. Once a container train is loaded (less than an hour in many cases), the power is attached to the head end, the brakes are pumped up, and the train heads out of town. What a great theme for a model railroad!

A GENERIC CONTAINER TERMINAL

The 11 x 20 around-the-walls track plan is designed to fit inside a one-car garage. A duckunder is needed to enter the

layout, which is schematically a continuous-run oval with a stub-ended branch that serves as the center of action—the container yard itself.

Of course, the biggest disadvantage to this layout is the need to duck under the benchwork. But depending on the position of the door, perhaps we can let our thinner operators, at least, take advantage of another Lionel modern-era accessory, the lift bridge, to get into and out of the operating area. Simply install a switch to control the bridge on the outside of the layout and you've converted the duckunder into a nod-under, or at least an interesting conversation piece. Those of us who long ago lost our youthful figures will have to contend with a conventional duckunder or risk becoming trapped in a narrow access aisle!

But once you get into the layout, this one will keep several operators busy for a few hours. Here's the basic scheme of operations: two crane operators keep loading and unloading stack trains as fast as the two road engineers can move the trains over the main line. It's up to your operators to set the pace, but there's no doubting the play value of the intermodal crane.

This plan is not inspired by one particular prototype facility, but represents a smattering of general principles.

A couple of holding tracks along one wall give an operator a place to hold trains, and give the crane crews a break! The onset of containerization hasn't completely eliminated conventional railroad equipment, so we've included a small town on one side of the layout that will give you a place to drop off and set out a boxcar, hopper, or two. And since commuter operations are so prevalent in and around cities that have large intermodal terminals, we have also included a passenger station and platforms for the travelers waiting to take the 5:15, or the Amtrak *Empire Builder*.

Make it big or small. Call it Chicago, Denver, or Los Angeles. No matter which prototype you chose, you'll find it exciting and interesting to feature the traffic and equipment that may have literally saved railroading.

Burlington Northern Trains

Diesel Engines

LION	8374	BN NW-2 Switcher, 83–85
LION	8585	BN SD-40 Twin Motors, 85
MTH	2045	BN SD-60M, 94
MTH	2067	BN GP-30, 95
RED	RC-15	BN GP-9, green, 94
WVR	1301	BN SD-40-2 "6773", 93
WMS	FP203	BN FP-45 Units, 95

Rolling Stock

LION	16217	BN Auto Carrier, white cover/screens, 92
LION	6427	BN Maintenance Caboose, 83–84
LION	9133	BN Flatcar w/ vans, 76–80
LION	16308	BN Flatcar w/ trailer, 88–89
MTH	9501	BN Husky-Stack Well Car, 96
ROW	383826	BN Well Car w/ containers, 93
ROW	383827	BN Well Car w/ containers, 94
WVR	U2507	BN 50' Flatcar, 95
LION	52014	BN TTUX Flatcar set w/ N&W trailers, 93
LION	52041	BN TTUX Flatcar set w/ Conrail trailers, 94
LION	52042	BN TTUX Flatcar set w/ CN trailer, 94

The centerpiece of White River Junction was, and still is, the attractive brick station. Central Vermont S-2 no. 7919 is pulling a Pullman, coach, and baggage car from B&M train 703 and will tack them on the end of the continuation of 703 bound for Berlin, New Hampshire, behind the Canadian Pacific 4-6-2 no. 2584. If you can't pick just one railroad, a junction will make an ideal prototype for your layout. Phil Hastings photo.

13 B&M and CV in the Land of Junctions

Junctions, places where the tracks of two or more railroads meet, or where a branch leaves the main line, are great places to watch railroad action. You can see locomotives and trains from each railroad that passes through the junction, and it's always a thrill to watch the trains set off and pick up cars. Few railfans would deny that New England, at least 40 to 50 years ago, was a land of junctions.

The six New England states were crisscrossed by hundreds of rail routes. Railroads came early to New England, and the Yankees took to them immediately. Before long, it seemed, virtually every village and hamlet in New England played host to a junction between two and more rail lines. And places where two railroads met that did not have a town didn't stay that way for long. To this day town names in Vermont, New Hampshire, Massachusetts, Connecticut, Maine, and Rhode Island end with the word "Junction." Among all those places, perhaps

Boston & Maine Track

Track
Lionel Single Straight (85)
Lionel O54 Curve (38)
Lionel O72 Right-Hand Turnout (9)
Lionel O72 Left-Hand Turnout (7)
Lionel O72 Curve 22.5° (18)
Lionel Custom-Cut Straight (12)
Lionel Half Straight (2)
Lionel Cut Stock Curve (2)
Lionel O42 Curve 30° (10)
Lionel O31 Modern Right-Hand Turnout (1)
Lionel O22 Left-Hand Turnout (1)
Lionel O22 Makeup Straight (1)

Structures
 1 Lionel 3462P Milk Car Platform (1)
 2 Lionel 138 Water Tower (1)
 3 Lionel 132 Passenger Station (1)
 4 Lionel 415 Diesel Fuel Station (1)
 5 Lionel 316/317 Trestle Bridge (1)
 6 Lionel 115 Lionel City Station (1)
 7 Lionel 156 Freight Platform (4)
 8 Lionel 314 Plate Girder Bridge (2)
 9 Lionel 12901 Steam Shovel (2)
10 Lionel 2175 Gravel Loader (1)

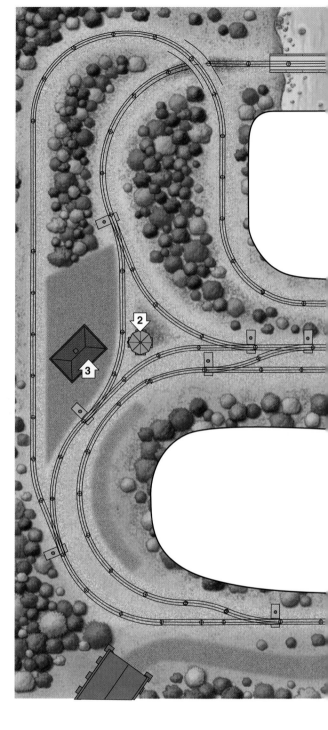

Boston & Maine 4-6-2 no. 3715 heads the *Northwind* south towards New York City. An F2 will follow the passenger train out of town on the point of freight JS4. Phil Hastings photo.

none was more famous among railfans than White River Junction.

CROSSROADS ON THE CONNECTICUT

Although it's no Mississippi, the Connecticut River was a significant artery of commerce in earlier times.

The river starts at the Canadian border and winds its way south, serving as the border between Vermont and New Hampshire before it bisects the states of Massachusetts and Connecticut. About halfway to Canada on Vermont's eastern border, the White River joins the Connecticut. Here the Boston & Maine and Central Vermont joined to create one of the most important rail junctions in

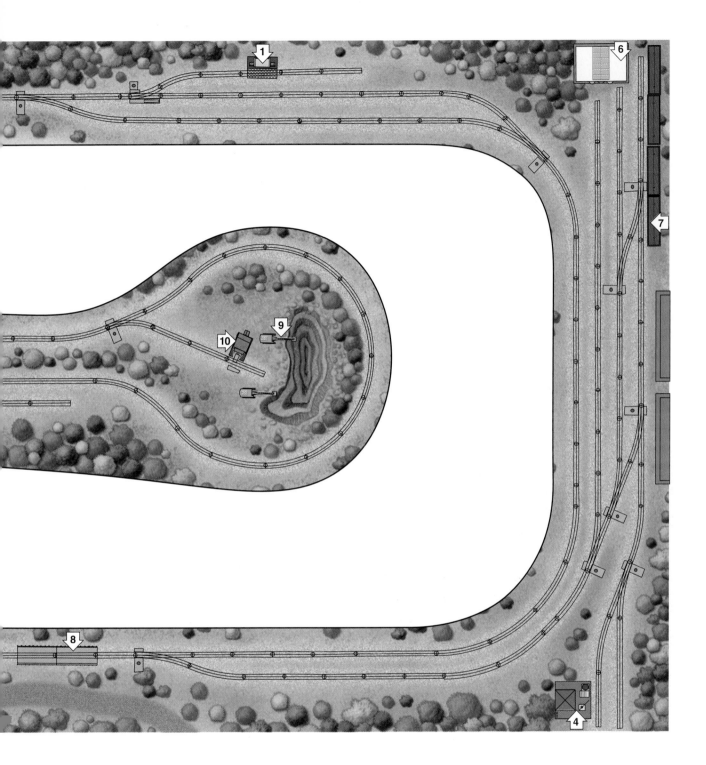

northern New England—aptly named White River Junction.

The centerpiece of White River Junction was, and still is, the handsome colonial brick station, which for years boasted a locomotive weathervane.

The station sat in the center of a wye track that served as the diverging routes of the B&M and CV. Both railroads main-tained yards and engine-servicing facilities in the area—the CV just north of the sta-tion, and the B&M across the Connecticut River in Walpole, New Hampshire. Junc-tions and small towns were a critical part of New England railroading, and are an essential part of the theme for this layout.

White River was also unique in that locomotives and passenger cars from every

If two railroads just aren't enough, how about a third? Canadian Pacific was a regular visitor to White River Junction, Vermont. Here, a pair of CP Alcos in classic maroon and gray livery lead a short freight out of White River Jct. The train is on B&M rails now, but will return to home rails in Wells River, just up the line. Phil Hastings photo.

Boston & Maine Trains

Steam Engines

WMS	5012	B&M USRA 4-6-2 Pacific, 89

Diesel Engines

LION	226	B&M Alco AB Units, white stripe/letters, 60
LION	8654	B&M GP-9 Powered, 76–77
LION	8655	B&M GP-9 Dummy, blue, white, 76–77
LION	18918	B&M NW-2 "8918", black frame, white lettering, 93
LION	18929	B&M Switcher Calf Unit, white letters, 95
MTH	2126	B&M F-3 AA Units, 96
MTH	2126B	B&M F-3 B Unit, 96
RED	RC-31	B&M GP-9, 94
RED	RC-75	B&M GP-9, early scheme, 94

Motorized Units

WMS	RDC208	B&M Budd RDC, set of 3, 96
3RD	No Number	B&M Flying Yankee, 96

Rolling Stock

LION	6464-475	B&M Boxcar, black/white lettering, 57–68
LION	9768	B&M Boxcar, black/white lettering, 76–77
LION	6017-100	B&M SP Caboose, 59–66
		(A) Light to medium blue
		(B) Purplish blue
LION	9181	B&M N5C Caboose, 76–77
LION	16911	B&M Flatcar w/ white trailer w/ B&M logo, 94
LION	16353	B&M Gondola w/ coil covers, 91
LION	16407	B&M Quad Hopper, black lettering (SSS), 91

Passenger Cars

WMS	M203	B&M Madison Passenger set, maroon, 94–95
WMS	SM203	B&M 72' Madison Passenger set, maroon, 95

major New England and Canadian railroad could be found in town. The Central Vermont was owned by the Canadian National Railway, so CN locomotives were commonly used on CV trains. The B&M and Canadian Pacific operated several joint trains that included power and equipment from both railroads, and it would regularly pass through town.

The 14 x 22-foot layout shown here centers on the wye-style junction. The layout includes the tracks of two railroads (or a main line and a branch) and you may want to use different ballast for each to make the two different railroads obvious.

At the junction, the two lines separate and the branch drops down and passes under the main line and heads out onto a narrow peninsula. The branch rejoins the main back at the junction. The peninsula serves a dual purpose: to appear as a second railroad and to give you a place to turn complete trains around. You'll have to watch what kind of equipment runs on the branch, since it doesn't share the broader O52 curves of the main line that loop around the walls of the room.

The rest of this layout can be scenicked as shown to reflect New England's unique appearance. Quarrying operations were an important traffic source for New England lines, and a Lionel gravel loader and a coupler of steam shovels form the centerpiece of a quarry. Milk was also once an important type of traffic in the region, and every line in the area operated fleets of milk cars.

In addition to a fair amount of postwar and MPC equipment for the Boston & Maine and Central Vermont, new manufacturers such as Red Caboose and MTH Electric Trains have offered hi-rail equipment lettered for these unique New England roads.

When it comes time to scenic the layout you'll need lots and lots of trees. While it's often easier to model New England in the summer, if you really want your visitors to walk away from the layout awestruck, consider depicting the rugged hillsides of New England ablaze in spectacular fall colors.

A mountainous wall between Mojave and Bakersfield, California, meant that the Southern Pacific had to loop up and over itself to gain sufficient elevation while minimizing the grades. For years the Tehachapi Loop has been a mecca for railfans and modelers. Perhaps it would make the perfect prototype for your next O gauge layout. Southern Pacific Lines photo.

14 Tehachapi
Prototype mountain railroading that looks like the work of a modeler

Tehachapi. In simple terms, it's the name given to the mountain grade used by the Southern Pacific and Atchison, Topeka & Santa Fe to climb over the Tehachapi Mountains and reach the Mojave desert. To true believers, railfans, model railroaders, and everyone in between, Tehachapi is spoken of in hushed, almost reverent tones.

But before we can design a layout that hopes to capture the spirit of Tehachapi, we need to examine the history of this unique stretch of railroad.

THE STRUGGLE TO GET OVER THE MOUNTAINS

The Tehachapi Mountains aren't especially tall, but they were tall enough to give the Southern Pacific fits when it built its coast line south to Los Angeles. The SP reached the small town of Caliente by 1875, and many would-be real estate barons purchased land in the town, figuring it would become the railroad's southern terminus. But they forgot to fill SP's assistant chief engineer, William Hood, in on that fact.

He surveyed a line that climbed to

Southern Pacific Track

Track
Lionel O72 Curve 22.5° (73)
Lionel 40-in. Straight (6)
Lionel O72 Right-Hand
  Turnout (10)
Lionel O54 Curve (26)
Lionel Half Straight (3)
Lionel Custom-Cut Straight (10)
Lionel Single Straight (28)
Lionel O42 Curve 30° (2)
Lionel O54 Half Curve (1)

Structures
1 Lionel 3656 Stockyard (1)
2 Lionel 12889 Motorized
  Windmill (1)
3 Lionel 12703 Icing Station (1)
4 Lionel 2140 Banjo Signal (2)
5 Lionel 12832 Block Signal (4)
6 Lionel 12848 Oil Derrick (1)
7 Lionel 12912 Pumping Station (1)
8 Lionel 2305 Getty Oil Derrick (1)
9 Lionel 12902 Marathon
  Oil Derrick (1)
10 Lionel 12718 Barrel Shed (1)
11 Lionel 12773 Freight Platform (1)
12 Lionel 12895 Double Signal
  Bridge (1)
13 Lionel 2300 Oil Drum Loader (1)

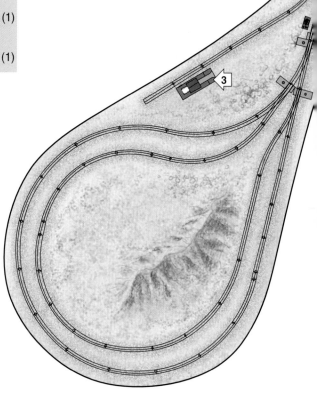

Tehachapi is also shared by trains of the Santa Fe. Here an AT&SF freight crosses up and over itself as it heads for Bakersfield. The tradition of lots of horsepower to climb the loop continues to this day. Donald Sims photo.

Mojave by doubling back on itself at Caliente. In the 7 miles of track from Caliente to Cliff, the railroad travels only a mile and gains over 700 feet in elevation. Two other horseshoe curves switch the direction of travel along the route, but the crowning genius of Hood's route is found just beyond Tunnel no. 9 where the main line makes a complete circle and crosses up and over itself to gain 77 feet of height. While the idea of using a loop to gain elevation and keep the grade within limits seemed obvious to Hood, it wasn't obvious to other locating engineers. Only a few other places have such loops, but generations of model railroaders have

been grateful to Mr. Hood for showing them that a loop up and over itself is, indeed, prototypical.

But don't think for a minute that this makes it easy to climb the loop. That minimum grade of 2 percent requires lots of horsepower to boost a train to the summit. In fact, it's not uncommon to see a train with 4 to 6 units on the head end, a quartet of helpers in the middle, and two pushers on the rear. This is mountain railroading with a capital "M."

MORE THAN ONE RAILROAD
But what if you don't like to limit your interests to just one railroad? That's okay.

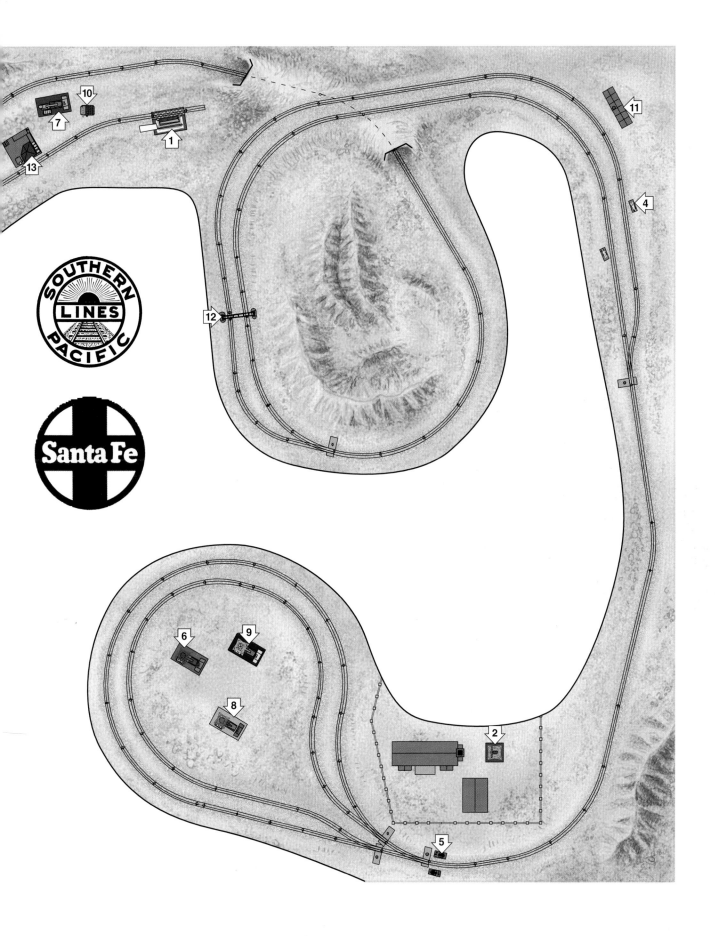

Even contemporary, high-horsepower diesel locomotives require the combined push-pull effort to conquer the loop. The second train traveling down the grade doesn't need any additional horsepower on the tail end, but certainly needs plenty of braking power!

Southern Pacific Trains

Steam Engines

LION	18007	SP GS-2 4-8-4 Steam Locomotive, 91
ROW	5201	SP 0-4-0 Saddle Tanker, 91
3RD	OG3RSPUP	SP 2-8-0 Consolidation, 95
WVR	1060	SP 4-8-4 GS-2, 93
WMS	5600	SP GS-4 4-8-4, orange, 89
WMS	7002	SP 4-8-8-2 Cab Forward, 90

Diesel Engines

LION	8960	SP U36C, pair, white lettering, 79
LION	18831	SP GP-20, red nose, white letters, "4060", 94
MTH	2112	SP SD-9, 96
RED	RC-11	SP GP-9, "black widow" scheme, 94
RED	RC-43	SP GP-9, gray/red, 94
3RD	No Number	SP Dash C44-9W, 96
3RD	No Number	SP AC 4400, 96
WVR	1332	SP U25B, 96
WVR	5518	SP RS-3, black "5545", 90
WMS	4107	SP FM Trainmaster Units, black, 90
WMS	SN209	SP Sharknose ABA Units, orange, 94

Motorized Units

WMS	BC206	SP Budd RDC, set of 3, 95

Rolling Stock

LION	X6454	SP Boxcar, light brown w/ white letters, 49–52
LION	9607	SP Hi-cube, white letters, 76–77
WMS	FC02	SP Boxcar, silver, 93–95
WMS	FC39	SP Boxcar, black, 93–95
LION	9316	SP Bay Window Caboose, 79
LION	16130	SP Stock Car (O27), 93–94
LION	16345/46	SP TTUX Trailer Train Car, yellow, 92
ROW	310128	SP Flatcars w/Ertl Tractors, 94
WVR	U2503	SP 50' Flatcar, 95
LION	9315	SP Gondola, white letters, 79
LION	19311	SP Covered Hopper, gray, 90
LION	16630	SP Operating Cowboy Stock Car, black lettering, 90–91

Passenger Cars

ROW	3501	SP Passenger Car, set of 6, 91
WVR	1106	SP Passenger Cars, set of 5, 9–93
WMS	LL611	SP 60' Passenger set, orange/red, 89–94

You can still model this region, since the Santa Fe shares the track up, over, and around Tehachapi. If that isn't enough, consider the following: the SP was purchased by the Denver & Rio Grande Western, so now you find Rio Grande tiger-stripe units on the loop. Let's face it—Tehachapi is a great place to watch trains, and you can make it a great place to watch trains in your basement.

THE LOOP TRACK PLAN

The loop itself is the centerpiece of this layout. Schematically, the rather large layout (20 x 26 feet) is a continuous-run configuration commonly called a loop-to-loop.

The mainline minimum radius is O72, meaning this layout can accommodate almost any of the larger steamers coming on the market, as well as the modern diesels available from manufacturers such as Lionel, MTH, and Third Rail.

There's not much evidence of civilization, but I've added a few accessories that wouldn't be too out of place on the layout. Tehachapi isn't the kind of place an accessory fanatic would choose as inspiration for a layout. This is a railroad for the modeler who wants to create some nice desert scenery and then sit back and watch as long trains slug their way over the mountain.

The sidings inside each reverse loop will let you hold two trains offstage. A third train can sit in the hole at the siding just below tunnel 9 as a fourth train winds its way up and over itself. And don't worry if the locomotives cross their own train on the way over the loop—the big boys do that all the time.

This is an ideal layout for the modeler who wants to model a real-world scene, but doesn't want to commit to a particular era. The loop is fairly timeless, so all you need to do is change the rolling stock and equipment to reflect 1949, 1965, or 1996.

One thing is for certain—visiting modelers and railfans will know what you're modeling almost immediately. That's the magic of Tehachapi.

The prototype for a Lionel O gauge model, two of the New Haven's ex-Virginian EF-4s are heading through Greens Farms, Connecticut, in February 1964. The New Haven's dense traffic and multitrack main line make it an ideal prototype for a toy train layout. John P. Ahrens photo.

15 The New Haven

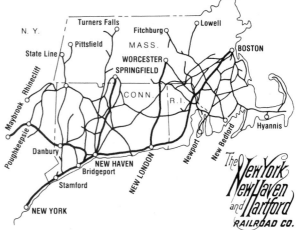

With the possible exception of the Pennsylvania Railroad, no other American railroad crammed as much traffic, trackage, or operations into as small an area as the New York, New Haven & Hartford. The routes of the New Haven were limited to the states of Connecticut, Massachusetts, and Rhode Island, along with a small corner of New York.

From New York City to New Haven the main line is a four-track electrified division that extends to New Haven. There the line splits, with two tracks heading for Boston and two north for Springfield.

A BRIEF HISTORY

The history of the New Haven is full of scandals, swindles, and scoundrels. Although more than a hundred individual companies made it the New Haven, the railroad really came into being in 1872 with the consolidation of the New York & New Haven and the Hartford & New Haven railroads. By 1893 the New York, New Haven & Hartford acquired the Old Colony Railroad, completing a New York–Boston main line.

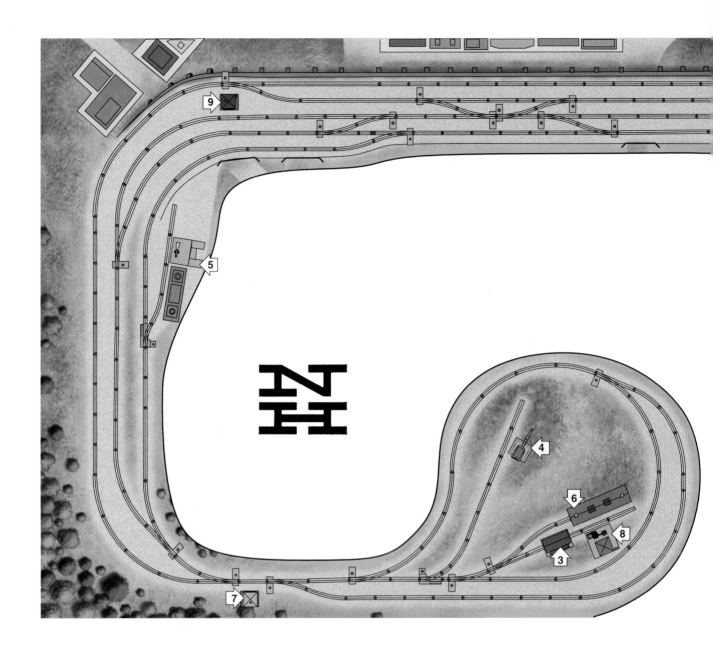

A railroad concentrated in the industrial areas of New England, with a main line linking two of the most important cities on the continent, didn't escape notice of the rail barons of the day. The New Haven soon came under the control

The New Haven served both of Manhattan's large passenger terminals—Grand Central and Penn Station. Penn station was reached by crossing the East River on the massive Hell Gate Bridge. EP-5 no. 371 is pulling the *William Penn* across Hell Gate in July 1955. Gary Gadziala photo.

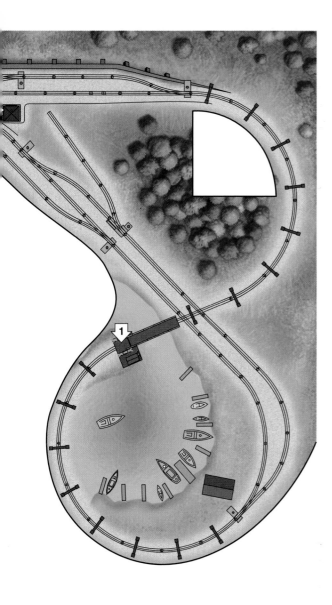

New Haven Track

Track
Lionel Single Straight (104)
Lionel O54 Curve (11)
Lionel O72 Curve 22.5 (71)
Lionel O72 Left-Hand Turnout (13)
Lionel 40-in. Straight (3)
Lionel O72 Right-Hand Turnout (11)
Lionel Half Straight (5)
Lionel Custom-Cut Straight (13)
Lionel O22 Right-Hand Turnout (2)
Lionel O22 Left-Hand Turnout (1)
Lionel O22 Makeup Straight (1)
Lionel O22 Makeup Curve (2)

Structures
1 Lionel 313 Bascule Bridge (1)
2 Lionel 445 Railroad Switch Tower (1)
3 Lionel 497 Coaling Station (1)
4 Lionel 182 Magnet Crane (1)
5 Lionel 460/461 Truck Platform (1)
6 Lionel 12897 Engine House (1)
7 Lionel 12917 Operating Switch Tower (1)
8 Lionel 12701 Fueling Station (1)
9 Lionel 12768 Burning Switch Tower (1)

New York, New Haven & Hartford Trains

Steam Engines
LION	8007	NYNH&H 2-6-4 Steam, gold stripe, 80–81

Diesel Engines
LION	8851/8852	NH F-3, AA, pair, 78–79
LION	18806	NH SD-18 diesel "8806", 89
MTH	2089	NH F-3 AA Units, 95
MTH	2097	NH F-3 B Unit, 95
RED	RC-81G	NH GP-9, 94
WVR	U6600	NH Alco FA-2 Unit, 90
WVR	U6601	NH Alco FB-2 Unit, 90
WMS	FM223	NH FM Trainmaster Units, 96
WMS	SD204	NH SD-45 Units, 95

Electric Engines
LION	8754	NH Rectifier, 77–78
WMS	EP200	NH EP-5 Units, 94–95

Motorized Units
WMS	RDC212	NH Budd RDC, set of 3, 96

Rolling Stock
LION	6464-425	NH Boxcar, orange door, 56–58
LION	6468-25	NH Auto Boxcar, black doors, 56–58
LION	9605	NH Hi-cube, black door, white lettering, 76–77
LION	16624	NH Cop and Hobo Operating Boxcar, 90–91
LION	17217	NH "State of Maine" Boxcar "45003" (Std O), 95
WMS	FC21	NH Boxcar, orange, 93–95
WMS	FC50	NH Boxcar, black, 93–95
LION	9272	NH Bay Window Caboose, 78–80
LION	9380	NH Caboose, black roof/lettering, 80–81

Passenger Cars
LION	16080	NH Baggage Car "6080", orange stripe, 95
LION	16081	NH Combo Car "6081", orange stripe, 95
LION	16082	NH Coach "6082", orange stripe, 95
LION	16083	NH Vista Dome Car "6083", 95
LION	16084	NH Full Vista Dome Car "6084", 95
LION	16086	NH Observation Car "6086", 95
WMS	M220	NH Madison Passenger set, black/orange, 94–95

of Charles Mellen, a protégé of the infamous J. P. Morgan. Mellen expanded New Haven's stranglehold on southern New England rail routes, and no branch line, interurban, or street railroad escaped his attention for long.

Although the New Haven was affected by the Great Depression in the 1930s, and even filed for bankruptcy in 1935, the railroad entered World War II leaner than ever before, getting rid of many redundant lines and adding some diesels to its rosters of electrics and steamers.

The railroad emerged from the Second World War in good shape physically and

The triangular catenary wire, the pagoda roof tower, and the four-track main line would tell us this is the New Haven, even if box-cab 311 weren't in the picture. Cos Cob, Connecticut, circa 1952. Fielding J. Boniman photo.

financially, and by 1947 the line was out of bankruptcy. But a combination of inexperienced and inept management and the completion of the Connecticut Turnpike, which virtually paralleled the New Haven between Boston and New York, caused the line to sink once again into the financial mires by the mid '50s. By 1961 the New Haven petitioned to be included in the New York Central–Pennsylvania Railroad merger. Despite some objections from the other two railroads, the New Haven disappeared into Penn Central on December 31, 1968. Today, much of the former New Haven's freight lines are operated by Conrail and other New England lines, and the four-track electrified division plays host to Metro-North commuter trains and is an important part of Amtrak's Northeast Corridor.

The New Haven was known for fast, frequent trains and multitrack main lines. Scattered along the main line were interlocking towers, and trains were routed from one track to the other by tower operators. One of these towers, with the attendant series of crossovers to let trains slip to any track, traveling in either direction, would be the perfect centerpiece of a New Haven layout.

Since the New Haven ran so many passenger trains (only the Long Island Railroad ran more passenger train miles than the NH), O72 seems to be required wherever possible. A small engine terminal where the builder can display a collection of diesel, electric, and steam motive power is another highlight of this 16 x 30-foot walk-in layout.

Westchester County, New York, and Fairfield County, Connecticut, play host to some of the nicest communities in the Northeast, and one lobe of the layout has a limited amount of track, so the builder can add a small Main Street scene, part of a golf course, or a small yacht club basin, as we've shown. Also, notice that the railroad runs above street level. There are no street crossings on the New Haven's main line, since the speed and frequency of the traffic would make them extremely dangerous.

While we could have a four-track main line throughout the layout, it would fill the space with track to the detriment of other scenic details. But there's no lack of trackage on this layout. The interlocking is the operational interest center. Its four O72 crossovers will let you and your visitors route and re-route the *Yankee Clipper,* the *Merchants Limited,* and all the other trains that passed through southern Connecticut every day as they rocketed their way towards New Haven and Boston. And those passenger trains weren't limited to New Haven equipment, either. Cars from every major U.S. railroad, including the Pennsylvania, New York Central, Union Pacific, and even the Santa Fe, regularly appeared in New Haven trains.

The truly brave and dedicated hi-railer will want to add catenary to the layout. Although the specifics are beyond the scope of this book, rest assured you can have those EP-5s running under wires like their big brothers did. More detailed information on installing overhead catenary is included in the Kalmbach publication, *Greenberg's Wiring Your Lionel Layout, Volume III: Advanced Technologies Made Easy.*

If you want to run fast, frequent trains and operate a wide range of all types of motive power (steam, diesel, and electric) the New Haven is a tough choice to beat.

This pair of CP SD40-2s look like models as they thread their way through Stoney Creek on the point of an empty coal drag. D. S. Harrop photo.

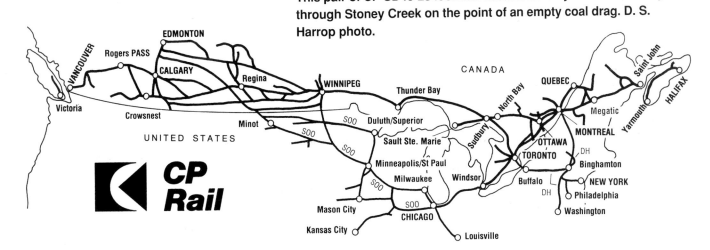

16 CP Rail in British Columbia

Today CP Rail is one of the most aggressive and successful railroads in North America, operating a 19,500-mile system that stretches from coast to coast in Canada. Through trackage rights and acquisitions of U.S. lines it stretches as far south as Washington, D.C., Kansas City, Missouri, and Louisville, Kentucky. Mileage trades and pooled operating agreements mean that any one of CPR's 1,669 locomotives can be seen at any time anywhere in North America.

CP Rail Track

Track
K-Line 14-in. Straight (16)
Lionel O72 Curve 22.5° (81)
Lionel Single Straight (45)
Lionel O72 Right-Hand Turnout (5)
Lionel O22 Right-Hand Turnout (1)
Lionel Custom-Cut Straight (10)
Lionel O72 Left-Hand Turnout (9)
Lionel Half Straight (6)
Lionel 40-in. Straight (12)
Lionel O22 Left-Hand Turnout (1)
Lionel O22 Makeup Curve (1)
Lionel O31 Curve 45° (1)

Structures
1 Lionel 315 Trestle Bridge (1)
2 Lionel 362 Barrel Loader (1)
3 Lionel 314 Plate Girder Bridge (1)
4 Lionel 364 Lumber Loader (1)
5 Lionel 264 Forklift Platform (1)
6 Lionel 12770 Arch-Under Bridge (1)
7 Lionel 12877 Illuminated Fueling Station (1)
8 Lionel 12741 UP Intermodal Crane (1)
9 Lionel 12734 Passenger/Freight Station (1)
10 Lionel 62709 Rico Station (1)
11 Lionel 12706 Barrel Loader (1)
12 Lionel 12905 Factory (1)
13 Lionel 2321 Sawmill (1)
14 Lionel/MPC 2301 Operating Sawmill (1)
15 Lionel 12705 Lumber Shed (2)
16 Lionel 12733 Watchman's Shanty (1)
17 Lionel 12916 Water Tower (1)
18 Lionel 12773 Freight Platform (1)
19 Lionel 2313 Floodlight Tower (3)
20 Lionel 12884 Truck Loading Dock (1)
21 Lionel 12906 Maintenance Shed (1)

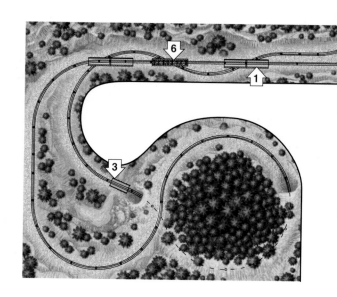

Snowdrifts can literally bury the main line through the mountains, making snowsheds like these at Laurie a necessity. D. S. Harrop photo.

The story of CP Rail starts in the late nineteenth century and was a direct result of the addition of British Columbia to the Canadian confederation in 1871. One stipulation of this political deal was completion of a rail link between the eastern part of Canada and British Columbia.

The new railroad faced challenges at least as hazardous as those experienced less than three years earlier by the first U.S. transcontinental route: harsh wilderness in northern Ontario, the vast expanse of prairie land, and the most formidable barrier of all, the Rocky Mountains.

Despite the physical and financial problems plaguing the project almost from the start, the completion of the Canadian Pacific Railway, as the line was called, soon became a matter of national pride. The railroad chose a far more difficult route along the north shore of Lake Superior to avoid an easier route that would have meant the main line would pass through U.S. territory.

When the line reached Kicking Horse Pass in British Columbia, engineers had to resort to a temporary 4.5 percent grade that was eventually replaced with a unique pair of spiral tunnels. Against all the odds and naysayers, the dream prevailed and the gold spike of the Canadian Pacific Railway was driven on November 5, 1885. Canada was truly united coast to coast.

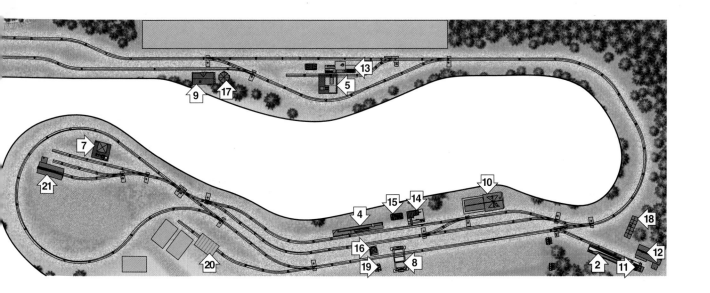

STEADY EXPANSION

Even before the driving of the gold spike, CP was already growing. The Canada Central Railway was absorbed into the system in 1881. CP entered Montreal by acquiring and extending the Ontario & Quebec Railway in 1884. By 1890 this line had been extended across the state of Maine to reach St. John, New Brunswick. That was the first time CP track crossed the U.S. border, but it was not the last.

The Minneapolis, St. Paul & Sault Ste. Marie Railway (Soo Line) came under CP control in the late 1880s, a control more obvious than ever today. Bankrupt Delaware & Hudson was acquired from Guilford Transportation in January 1991, specifically for the D&H's access to the U.S. capital.

Today, CP Rail operates the lines of the Soo, D&H, and its own holdings as an integrated system. Modern motive power, aggressive marketing, and fascinating operations make it easy to settle on CP Rail as a prototype. And when it comes time to choose a setting for a CP Rail layout, one location surfaces as ideal: Kicking Horse Pass, and the spiral tunnels.

SPIRAL TUNNELS

The famed spiral tunnels were carved from the rock of Cathedral Mountain and

Canadian Pacific Trains

Steam Engines

WVR	1074	CP 4-6-4 Royal Hudson, 94

Diesel Engines

LION	2373	CP F-3 AA Units, yellow trim, 57
LION	8152	CP SD-24 Powered, 81
LION	18203	CP Rail SD-40 "8203", 89
MTH	2046	CP Rail SD-60M, 94
RED	RC-39	CP GP-9, maroon/gray, 94
WVR	1034	CP E-8 AA Units "1800" & "1801", 92
WVR	1324	CP Rail SD-40-2 "6034", 95
WMS	5849	CP Rail SD-45, 84
WMS	FP204	CP FP-45 Units, 95

Motorized Units

LION	8264	CP Snowplow, yellow lettering, 82
LION	18411	CP Fire Fighter Car, Powered, 90

Rolling Stock

LION	9208	CP Rail Boxcar, black lettering, 71
LION	17200	CP Boxcar (Std O), 89
LION	19207	CP Rail DDBoxcar, burnt orange, 88
LION	5728	CP Bunk Car, white letters, 86
LION	9165	CP N5C Caboose, white lettering (SSS), 73
LION	19705	CP Rail Wide-vision Caboose, 89
WMS	FC07	CP Stock Car, Tuscan red, 93–95
LION	6508	CP Crane, 12-wheel, 81
LION	6233	CP Flatcar w/ stakes (Std. O), 86
LION	16395	CP Flatcar w/ rail load, red, white lettering, 94
LION	16903	CP Bulkhead Flatcar w/ pulp load (SSS), 94
LION	17500	CP Rail Flatcar w/ logs (Std O), 89
LION	9336	CP Rail Gondola, white lettering, 79
LION	17400	CP Rail Gondola w/ coal load (Std O), 89
LION	9017	CP Short Hopper, gold lettering, 71
LION	5710	CP Woodside Reefer, 82–83
LION	17300	CP Reefer (Std O), 89

Passenger Cars

LION	2551	Banff Park Observation, maroon stripe, 57
LION	2552	Skyline 500 Vista Dome, maroon stripe, 57
LION	2553	Blair Manor Pullman, maroon stripe, 57
LION	2554	Craig Manor Pullman, maroon stripe, 57
WMS	M206	CP Madison Passenger set, maroon, 95

Rugged scenery that dwarfs the trains and brightly painted motive power and equipment make CP Rail in the Canadian Rockies an excellent choice for a prototype. T. O. Repp photo.

Mt. Ogden between 1907 and 1908. A 900-foot vertical drop in only four miles was the reason for the loop tunnel inside a mountain. Just as the Southern Pacific had to loop up and over itself at Tehachapi to gain elevation, CP decided on the same solution to a similar problem. The only difference was that CP was deep in the heart of a mountain range, meaning the tunnel had to be curved and on a grade inside the rock.

The plan here was designed for a basement with a long, narrow area for the layout. The final plan features two distinct areas: a city or town area to the right of the door, which serves as the operating interest center of the layout, and the spiral tunnel scene, which naturally enough provides the scenic highlight for the layout.

The finished design features a small yard with an intermodal loading area and a small engine-service facility. (Those mountain grades require lots of power.) After leaving town, we pass through some typical scenery before arriving in a small lumbering community, which is an ideal place to locate a sawmill. The main line splits at this point and proceeds into the mountain areas. Highlights of this section of the layout are the snowsheds, the tunnel itself, and a long, high bridge guaranteed to quicken the pulse of any engineer.

After completing the hair-raising trip through the mountains, the main rejoins itself and heads back to the small yard, making this an out-and-back schematic. A reverse loop at one end of the yard, cleverly masked by town buildings on the hillside, serves to turn locomotives or entire consists.

CP Rail locomotives and rolling stock are quite colorful, and as such they make excellent prototypes for toy train manufacturers. Lionel and MTH both have a roundhouse full of Action Red locomotives from which to choose. Soo Line Red locomotives could also be in these 1:48 scale Rockies. The table shows some other interesting equipment that can call this layout home.

Floor-to-ceiling scenery, colorful trains, and a historic sight familiar to all North American railfans mean you may want to look north of the border for the prototype for your next layout.